THIS IS
NAMIBIA

THIS IS
NAMIBIA

Gerald Cubitt · Peter Joyce

NEW
HOLLAND

First published in the UK in 1992 by
New Holland (Publishers) Ltd
Garfield House, 86—88 Edgware Road,
W2 2EA London, United Kingdom
www.newhollandpublishers.com

New Holland Publishing is a member of the Johnnic Publishing Group

Second UK edition 1999

10 9 8 7 6 5 4 3 2

Project Co-ordinator: Marje Hemp
Designer: Odette Marais
Cover designer: Tracey Mackenzie
Typesetting by Struik DTP, Cape Town
Reproduction by Unifoto (Pty) Ltd, Cape Town
Printed and bound Times Offset (M) Sdn Bhd

ISBN 1 85974 268 8

PHOTOGRAPHER'S ACKNOWLEDGEMENTS
I would like to thank the many people and organisations who assisted
me during my stay in Namibia, in particular: The Namibian Ministry of
Information and Broadcasting; Kalahari Sands Hotel (Sun International)
in Windhoek; Namib Sun Hotels: Mokuti Lodge (Etosha), Strand Hotel
(Swakopmund), Hotel Eckleben (Tsumeb), Hotel Hamburger Hof and
Otjiwa Game Ranch (Otjiwarongo), Hansa Hotel (Keetmanshoop);
CDM (Pty) Ltd (Oranjemund and Navachab); Rössing Uranium Ltd;
Tsumeb Mining Corporation; Lianshulu Lodge; Zambezi Lodge;
Okonjima Guest Farm; Mount Etjo Safari Lodge, Desert Adventure Safari;
Johan Nel; Braam Naudé; Grant Burton and Marie Holstenson; Val,
Rose and Wayne Hanssen; Tryg and Trish Cooper; Amelia and Strydom
van der Wath; and Chris Eyre, Nature Conservation Officer at Opuwo.

FRONT COVER: *A hardy inhabitant of the Namib Desert, the gemsbok.*
SPINE PICTURE: *A Herero woman and her child.*
OPPOSITE: *Early morning in Lüderitz, a quaint German-style town*
surrounded by barren desert.

Log on to our photographic website **www.imagesofafrica.co.za**

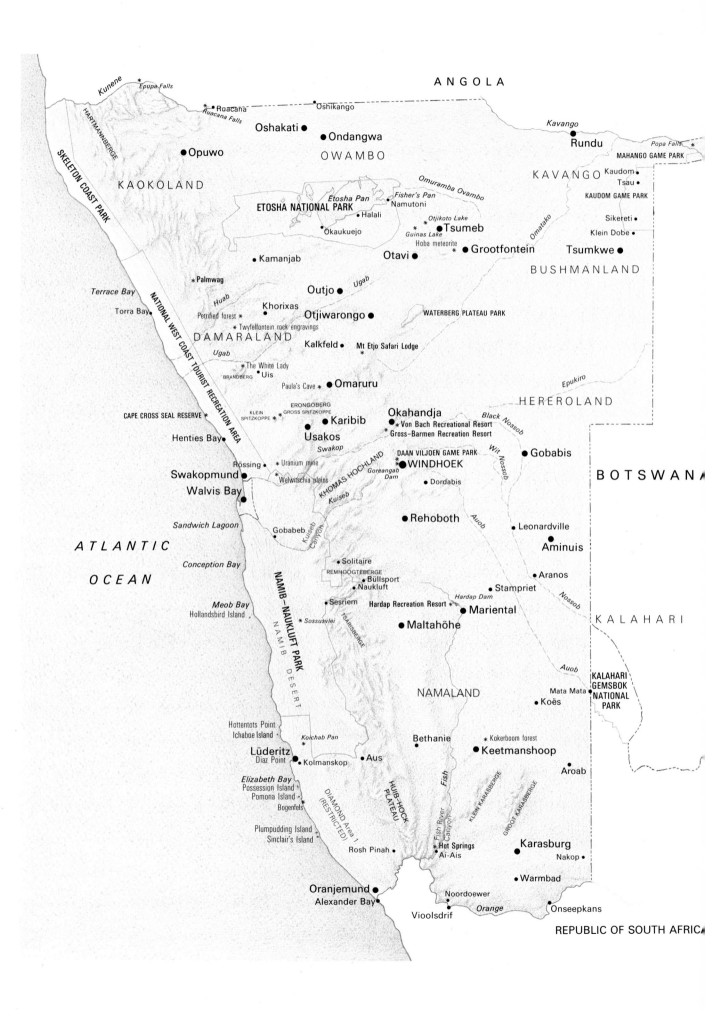

NAMIBIAN PROFILE

Namibia is a vast and mostly desolate territory that sprawls over the southwestern regions of the southern African subcontinent. Bisected by the Tropic of Capricorn, the country is bordered in the west by a forbidding 1 500-kilometre Atlantic coastline, in the north by the Kunene and Okavango rivers (beyond which are the republics of Angola and Zambia), in the east by Botswana, and in the southeast and south by the Republic of South Africa.

Included within Namibia's generally straight boundaries are two geographical and historical oddities. The Caprivi Strip is a long, narrow stretch of land (482 kilometres long and between 35 and 80 kilometres wide) that looks like a probing finger reaching eastward to and along the Zambezi River from the country's northeastern region, with its extremity close to the meeting point of three neighbouring states. Zambia, Zimbabwe and Botswana come together at the small town of Kazungula, and the common border of the last two countries is, at 45 metres, the shortest of the world's international frontiers.

Caprivi is one of the more curious relics of that extraordinary flurry of European expansionist activity known as the Scramble for Africa, and is testimony of an attempt by the 19th-century German imperialists to link their western and eastern possessions in Africa by means of a 1 500-kilometre cross-continental corridor – a hugely ambitious aspiration but, in the context of those grandly acquisitive times, one that wasn't entirely beyond the realms of possibility.

Walvis Bay, on the western seaboard, is also a hangover from the early colonial era. The bay, which provides a well-protected anchorage on a coast not noted for its natural harbours, was annexed to the British Crown in 1878, and in 1884 became an integral part of the Cape Colony. The strategic, economically valuable enclave of 1 124 square metres in extent lying roughly midway between the Orange and Kunene rivers is still an integral part of South Africa, though legal title to the area is in dispute.

Namibia is 824 269 square kilometres in extent, 1 320 kilometres long from north to south, and from 400 kilometres to 1 000 kilometres wide (excluding the Caprivi Strip) from west to east. It is a big country, even by African standards; larger than Texas, about four times the size of the United Kingdom, and 27 times the size of Belgium. It is also a sparsely populated one: the total of its culturally diverse peoples stands at just 1,5 million, some 150 000 of whom live in and around the capital, Windhoek.

THE LAND

This is a country of immense solitude, of far horizons, arid deserts and jagged mountain heights, hauntingly beautiful in its stark emptiness, unforgiving in the harshness of its climate and terrain.

In some places the soils are surprisingly rich, but the rains are seldom generous, drought is the norm, and most of the great sunlit spaces are able to sustain only the hardier forms of plant and animal life.

The lie of the land

In the broadest physiographic terms Namibia comprises three distinct regions. A high central plateau runs like a spine from the southern to the northern borders of the country, and this is bordered on either side by deserts: the Kalahari to the east and the Namib of the coastal plain to the west.

The Namib is a long and narrow desert (the world's oldest), extending almost 2 000 kilometres from the Orange River northwards to the Kunene and beyond to Namibe in Angola, and inland to an average width of 150 kilometres. The terrain rises steadily inland until, at an altitude of around 1 000 metres, it reaches the edge of the central plateau.

The desert has many faces. In the south it is a sea of sand, of massive, regimented, shifting dunes, some of them a full 30 kilometres long and nearly 250 metres high. Here and there among them lies the odd salt pan or mud flat, relic of a sporadic stream that tried, and failed, to make its way to the ocean. Underground rivers cross the wasteland, their dry beds incongruously but refreshingly mantled in greenery. Farther north, the land levels to a harder plain from which the occasional isolated granite mountain rises, and the bedrock of which is slashed by deep gorges. There is little soil here, and what there is tends to be confined to the few floodplains and river estuaries of the area. Here, too, are the desolate shores of the Skeleton Coast, graveyard of a thousand ships and named for the many mariners who survived the wrecks only to perish in the desert wastes.

The plateau. To the east of the Namib coastal belt are the highlands of the central plateau, a hardveld tableland varying in height from 900 metres to nearly 2 000 metres.

This is a region of wide geophysical diversity: the countryside ranges from

Ox-wagons take 19th-century traders across the ruggedness of the south-central interior.

broken veld through sandy valleys and undulating plains to mountain massifs and jagged peaks.

Around Windhoek in the central segment the hills are especially noteworthy: the Auasberge (whose Moltkeblick, at 2 482 metres, is the country's second highest peak after the Brandberg, the Khomas Hoghland, the Onyati, the Eros and other ranges combine to form Namibia's highest tract of territory, a central watershed from which headwaters drain to all points of the compass. Much farther to the south is the plateau's most spectacular natural feature, the 161-kilometre-long Fish River Canyon.

The northern section is a distinctive region, quite different in character from the rest of the plateau. For the most part it comprises a great alluvial plain created by the Okavango and other rivers that flow southwards from Angola to feed the wetlands of northern Botswana and the huge, shallow depression known as the Etosha Pan. This is also upland country (900 to 1 200 metres), generally well watered and blessed with good grazing.

The highlands are the economic as well as the geographic heart of the country, enjoying relatively generous summer rains that sustain nutritious ground cover, flocks of karakul sheep and, in the north, cultivated lands and herds of beef and dairy cattle.

The Kalahari, part of southern Africa's great interior plateau, is more than 1,2 million square kilometres in area, covers most of Botswana, and extends into Zimbabwe, Zambia and Angola. It also stretches into Namibia, across the country's eastern border, to a depth of between 400 kilometres in the north and 80 kilometres in the south. It is commonly termed a desert, principally because its porous, sandy soils cannot retain surface water, but in reality much of it is formally classed as life-sustaining wilderness, and its sparsely grassed plains are home to huge numbers of game and other animals.

Climate

Namibia's climate falls into the 'continental tropical' category, though there is in fact very little of the steamy lushness that one associates with the latter word. It is indeed a hot country, but for the most part bone dry.

The rains, such as they are, fall during the summer months (November to February) in all areas except the extreme southwest, which sometimes enjoys a few, rather insignificant winter showers and, remarkably, the very occasional snowfall. Mean annual precipitation is about 250 millimetres, though the arid Lower Orange and Namib regions enjoy less than 100 millimetres a year and frequently a lot less. The dunes of the desert are subject to abrupt periods of heavy downpours and sudden flood, but these are few and far between in terms of both time and space, and some areas receive no rain at all for years on end.

The central and northern, and especially the northeastern, parts are better endowed, receiving up to 660 millimetres of precipitation during a good year, most of the moisture being brought by northerly and northeasterly winds.

The higher-lying areas tend to be a little wetter than the lower ones as the air is forced to rise and thus surrenders its moisture more readily.

The figures are deceptive, however. Apart from the regularly watered northern Owambo region (where, though there have been savage droughts in recent years, crop failures are generally rare), Namibia's rains are extraordinarily unreliable. Some of the drier parts receive their full annual quota (the recorded average) during a single cloudburst, and sometimes they get rather more. For example, in 1960 double the annual mean of 250 millimetres fell in just twelve hours at Uhlenhorst, drowning nearly all the domestic and many of the wild animals on a number of surrounding farms. Moreover, the rains tend to be a lot less beneficial than the recorded volumes may suggest, even taking into account their irregularity, as they fall during the hottest months and much of the moisture is therefore lost through evaporation (Namibia's surface water is siphoned off at an average rate of over two metres a year).

Temperatures vary according to area but are generally lower than those of other regions of the world that lie between the same lines of latitude. The climate in the desert coastal belt is largely determined by interaction between the upwelling of the cold Benguela Current offshore and the South Atlantic high pressure system, and the mean annual temperature along the often chilly and fogbound western seaboard hovers around a modest 16 °C.

Inland, across the central highlands, it ranges between 19 °C and 22 °C.

But these are averages, and they say little about the weather conditions you're likely to enjoy (or suffer) on any given day. High summer can be exceptionally hot, the temperature climbing to 40 °C and more in the north (Grootfontein is one of the hottest of the major centres) and to a fearsome 48 °C in the relentlessly shadeless Namib.

Water in a dry land

The country's perennial rivers are the Orange, Kunene, Okavango, Zambezi and Chobe, each of which functions as a national frontier with limited irrigation potential. Furthermore their waters are capable of enriching only the extreme southern and northern regions. There are one or two major rivers such as the Fish, the westward-flowing Swakop and Kuiseb and the shallower, eastward-flowing Omuramba, Omatako, and Epukiro, but they are intermittent and contain surface water only after the coming of the rains and floods. There is good ground water, though, beneath and around the riverbeds.

What above-ground moisture there is resides in shallow clay or limestone depressions, most of them in the sandveld semi-desert and some of quite prodigious dimensions. The largest of these is the renowned Etosha Pan.

The country is also blessed with a number of highly productive perennial springs and artesian wells.

Overall Namibia is grievously short of natural surface water resources, and in every part of the country except Owambo and Caprivi in the far north there is heavy reliance on boreholes and man-made dams, of which over 10 000 have been constructed. The largest is the Hardap Dam, in the south-central region.

Vegetation

Climate, and to a somewhat lesser degree geology and altitude, prescribe the nature of Namibia's major vegetation regions, of which there are four, together with a number of transitional zones.

The desert regions of the western seaboard are too dry to support any but the toughest and most adaptive of life forms such as lichens, a few dwarf shrub species on the otherwise barren flats, the distinctive quiver tree (*Aloe dichotoma*) or kokerboom – a slow-growing, gracefully shaped succulent that derives its common name from the use to which the Bushman (San) hunters put its branches – and the Namib's famed *Welwitschia mirabilis,* an unlikely, even bizarre plant that has evolved in quite remarkable fashion in order to survive in its ferociously hostile environment. Towards the east, as the land rises and the rains become a little more accommodating, one finds a greater number and variety of succulents and, in wetter periods, a thin grass cover.

All in all this is hardly an eye-catching array of floral splendour, but then the Namib's attractions lie elsewhere, in its monochromatic vastness, in the stark, clean outlines of dunes and outcrops, in its explosive dawns and sunsets, in its infinite stillness. However, plant life does have its brief moment of glory when the rare rains come and the long-dormant seeds of the desert annuals germinate, quickly taking advantage of the hour, and for a few days exquisitely decorating the sandy wastes with their blooms.

The highlands. The central plateau region is predominantly acacia country, the common species of which include the tree-like berg-thorn (*Acacia hereroensis*), the kudubush (*Combretum apiculatum*), the withoek in the more mountainous parts, the camelthorn (*A. erioloba*), the karee, the buffalo-thorn and the ana tree in the valleys of the Swakop, Kuiseb and Omaruru rivers. The uplands are moderately well grassed.

The Karstveld of the north is that portion of mountainous country encompassing southern Ovamboland and the Kaokoveld in the far northwest. Here you see stem succulents and a great many tree species, among them white seringa (*Kirkia acuminata*), marula *(Sclerocarya caffra)*, the African blackwood, also called the weeping bush, and in a wide area covering most of the Kaokoveld and parts farther east, the mopane and thick perennial grasses of the classic African savanna.

The Kalahari. As mentioned, this region falls well short of being a true desert. Most of its Namibian section is categorized as tree savanna, much of the southern segment being taken up by camel-thorn, red ebony and other acacias, and towards the centre by silver terminalia trees and shrubs.

Farther north, where the climate is wetter, the acacia gives way to bush savanna and dry woodland of Transvaal and Rhodesian teak (kiaat and mkusi respectively), Rhodesian ash (wild seringa), manketti, shiwi and other splendid timber species. Great numbers of tamboti trees grow around Grootfontein (where there are sawmills) and Tsumeb. These comparatively young forests support a lucrative timber industry with a good potential for expansion, as many of the woods have a beautiful grain and are much in demand by furniture-makers. On the wide plains of Owambo in the extreme north the forests thin out, to be replaced by mopane and makalani palm, wild fig and ancient baobab.

Wildlife

Namibia has a rich diversity of wildlife, ranging from conventional big game down to some invertebrate and lower vertebrate species that have adapted marvellously to their environment. Generally speaking, animal life in the northern parts is classed as tropical and that in the southern areas rather loosely as 'Cape fauna'.

Especially fascinating are the small, specialized animals, reptiles and insects of the Namib strip, some of them unique, living as they do in a desert that is old enough to have given free rein to the evolutionary process. For example beetles such as the toktokkie, and lizards, have adapted to sand-digging (among other things they have spines on their toes) and sand-diving. Other animals that live in this environment include chameleons, spiders, dune-locusts, adders and golden moles. Much of this life is sustained not by rain, as there's very little of this precious commodity in the desert, but by

the ocean mists and moisture-bearing sea winds, and by breezes from the interior that bring in dead leaves, grass segments and other nutritious bits and pieces. Larger game is sustained by the occasional pan and spring and by the vegetation that fringes the dry river-beds. Apart from the Cape fur seals, one of the coast's most frequently seen animals is the beach-combing jackal. Among the more prominent of the region's birds are the Dune Lark, the Tractrac Chat and bustards.

The bigger game species of the interior plateau include elephant, rhino, giraffe, lion and leopard, buffalo, gemsbok, eland, kudu, hartebeest, zebra and numerous other grazers, browsers and carnivores. The wildlife is perhaps at its most impressive in the Etosha National Park which, together with other major wilderness areas, is covered in some detail on pages 17 and 18.

THE PEOPLE

The country's population in 1991 was estimated at 1,4 million, translating into an average density of just under 1,5 persons per square kilometre, a figure that reflects the harsh nature of the land (only one per cent of its surface is arable). Namibia ranks as the 15th largest of Africa's states in area and is fully two thirds the size of neighbouring South Africa, yet the latter country – which is by no means a very crowded one by world standards – supports something like 30 times more people.

About one in four Namibians live in urban areas, and Windhoek is by far the largest centre. Countrywide, the natural rate of increase hovers around the three-per-cent mark and urban growth, fueled by a relentless drift from the countryside, is increasing at about twice that rate.

Despite the small number of people, Namibia's ethno-linguistic tapestry is richly coloured and remarkably intricate. The country is home to fully a dozen cultural groupings, each with its distinctive character and its own heritage. From largest to smallest, they are:

The Wambo, who comprise eight subgroups, together totalling nearly 600 000 people (just under half the country's population) and are concentrated in the far northern areas that stretch from the Kaokoveld in the west to Kavango in the east – a region known as Owambo. This is plains country, a flat, stoneless grassland crossed by sporadically rain-filled watercourses or *oshanas* and man-made feeder canals that, together, sustain dairy cattle and goats and good crops of maize, millet, pumpkins and melons.

The Wambo are a matrilineal people (succession is through the mother's line), and their basic social unit is the family group, each with its own village (*eumbo*), its own land and often its own waterhole. Traditionally the village is enclosed by a pole fence, within which there are fenced-off areas delineating the various functional parts. Among these are the sleeping quarters (usually rondavel-type huts), storage for wheat, milk, beer (*omalodu*), places for cooking, eating and working, the cattle-pen and so forth. Central to the larger village unit is the large open 'reception area' where feasts are held, visitors entertained and the 'holy fire' (sometimes simply a smouldering log) burns ceaselessly.

The ancient body of religious belief involves a Supreme Being (*Kalunga*) and the veneration of ancestors, but today little of the traditional religion remains today, as the majority of Wambo follow the Christian teachings of the Finnish Mission, which arrived in force in 1870. Most of the remainder are either Roman Catholics or Anglicans.

The Kavango people number some 110 000, most of whom live within a 40 000-square-kilometre area of the northeast, south of the Okavango River. This is a fairly flat, and high (1 100 metres) parklike region of tall grasses interspersed with scrub and patches of woodland that, towards the east, thicken into forests of mopane, mahogany, blackwood and teak (in all, over 200 tree and bush species have been identified). This is big game country, and the animal life includes elephant and buffalo, large buck and, in the River, crocodile, hippo and tigerfish.

The Kavango, divided into six tribal groups, are also a matrilineal people. Most of the rural families subsist on the cereals they grow and the livestock they raise, and on the fish of the river and its seasonal floodplains. Many are river dwellers, their most prized possession being a dugout canoe. Woodcarving is a flourishing local industry.

The Hereros, and their cousins the Mbanderu, inhabit the arid eastern sandveld areas abutting Botswana. The Himba, an offshoot, live in the Kaokoveld region in the north-west. Together, the three groups total some 90 000 individuals.

Until the early years of the century the Herero were nomadic pastoralists, living fairly comfortably off the meat and milk of the large herds of cattle, goats and sheep that grazed the pastures of Namibia's central upland region. However, after bloody battles with German colonial forces they were decimated and impoverished, and became translocated. Today cattle, nurtured by boreholes drilled in the sun-blasted sand and scrub of their new 'homeland', are still central to the local economy, but many Herero now raise sheep and poultry and grow subsistence crops of maize, millet and cowpeas. Rural groups are traditionally organized around an extended family based on patrilineal descent, though matrilineal elements are also recognized.

In visual terms the most remarkable Herero characteristic is the 'traditional' costume worn by the women: a long, colourful Victorian-type dress adapted from the styles favoured by the wives of early European missionaries.

The related Tjimba and Himba, whose home is the Kaokoveld, are highly distinctive sub-groups. The forebears of the latter were in fact Herero herders who were dispossessed by Nama warriors during the 19th century and fled to the remote and inhospitable northwestern region, where they became known as the ovaHimba (which means, roughly, 'beggars'). Over the ensuing decades these semi-nomadic pastoralists clung to their traditional ways, tenaciously shunning the trappings of 'civilization'.

The Damara, or Bergdama, are 90 000 strong and concentrated in the hinterland of the northeastern seaboard. They are something of a mystery as they speak a Khoikhoin language (see 'Nama' below) but in their appearance and culture are more akin to the negroid peoples of West and Central Africa. Their origins are obscure, and all that is known with certainty is that they brought with them the arts of pottery and iron-forging. The products of these were supplied to the dominant Herero and Nama.

The aboriginal Damara were organized in small migratory groups, each controlled by a chief who was advised by elder male kinsmen. Like the Wambo, they hold fire to be sacred, and other traditional religious beliefs encompass a Supreme Being responsible for the coming of the rains and the renewal of the earth.

Namibians of European origin number about 75 000, two thirds of whom are

Samuel Maherero, legendary leader of the Herero in their bitter wars against the Nama.

Afrikaans-speaking and a quarter German-speaking. The majority live in the urban centres of the central and southern regions and most are involved in commerce, manufacturing, the cattle and karakul sheep industries and, to a decreasing extent, in the civil administration.

The Nama, many of whom live in the central region south of Windhoek, are among the very last substantial groups of the true Khoikhoi (once called Hottentot).

By tradition the Nama are semi-nomadic pastoralists who originally occupied the country to the north and south of the Orange River, living a peaceful enough existence in the southern interior of today's Namibia, in 'Great Namaqualand', or Namaland – until the arrival, in the latter part of the 18th century, of the Herero, when competition for the life-sustaining grazing lands led to decades of bitter warfare. Later came the mixed-descent Oorlams groups, whose presence initially intensified the conflict but who eventually assumed the leadership of the Nama and carried on the struggle against the Herero. Later still, first under German and then under South African colonial rule, the Nama were confined to certain areas of the south-central region and their pastoral rights guaranteed within this area.

The Nama have much in common with the San, sharing with the latter their linguistic roots and to some degree their physical appearance as well. Both are light-skinned and fine-boned, though the Nama tend to be taller. Individual families still follow the old wandering ways, but most of the country's 60 000 Nama now live in permanent settlements and work within the formal economy. Most, too, have adopted Western lifestyles and the Christian religion.

Mixed-descent (or 'coloured') Namibians, who number about 50 000, are for the most part descendants of immigrants from the old Cape Colony. The majority are urban and Afrikaans-speaking.

The East Caprivian communities of the northeastern extension of Namibia bordering on Angola, Zambia and Botswana are closely related to the Lozi of Barotseland, a region of Zambia seasonally flooded by the waters of the mighty Zambezi river. Fishing, and to a degree hunting, are significant but by no means exclusive elements of the local economy – Caprivians also keep cattle and cultivate the land (maize, cereals, cassava and melons are among the crops).

Those living in the eastern segment of the 'Strip' lead a less permanent existence as they are displaced by the river's floodwaters for some months each year. Here the terrain is especially difficult for the traveller, for the roads are few and rudimentary, and the dense riverine cover of reeds and forest, the sandbanks and the marshes, tend to discourage all but the most intrepid visitors.

The East Caprivian population numbers around 45 000 and the principal administrative centre is Katima Mulilo on the Zambezi River.

The San or Bushmen are related to the Khoikhoi (see Nama above). By tradition they are hunter-gatherers, confined by tribal pressures and European settlement to the more inhospitable parts of the subcontinent.

The aboriginal Bushman culture centres on the small, nomadic, independent and essentially leaderless band or clan of families, usually comprising between 30 and 60 individuals who are bound by the ties of kinship. The clan's existence was governed by the seasons, by the movement of game and by the local availability of honey and the roots and fruits of desert plants.

The traditional San were superb trackers, and patient ones too, sometimes following a herd for many days before moving in close enough to use their bows and arrows. When the selected animal had been killed, the whole group joined in the feast, singing and dancing in trance-like ritual around the fire (San music is based on an atonal scale, and is as unique to these gentle people as is their language). When game was scarce, the group split up into smaller parties to search for food. In times of severe, prolonged drought the women chewed the bark of a particular tree which acts as a contraceptive, so preventing an increase in the number of mouths to feed. In especially hard times snakes, lizards and even scorpions were added to the diet.

During droughts and in the driest of the desert areas, the San stored water in ostrich shells, which they buried deep below the sandy surface. The shells were also used for making beads which, with the skin karosses, loin cloths and aprons, were the only adornments. The wandering lifestyle precluded ownership of anything that is not easy to carry, and shelters were rudimentary affairs of sticks, sometimes (among the southern clans) covered with reed mats.

That the San inhabited most of southern Africa in times long past is evident from the marvellously animated rock and cave paintings that are found as far afield as the Drakensberg, the southern Cape and in the semi-deserts of the northwestern subcontinent.

Namibia's 34 000 San comprise three groups: the Heikum of the area bordering the Etosha Pan, the !Khung (the prefix denotes a click sound) in the Kalahari sands of the northeast, and the Barakweno, who live along the Okavango River and in Western Caprivi. The clans are now less nomadic than their forbears, their members being settled in villages. Some of the San lead a pastoral existence, others work for wages, principally on the extensive stock farms of the interior.

The Basters, 30 000 in number, are a racially mixed, Westernized, Afrikaans-speaking people who arrived from the Cape Colony in the late 1860s, bringing with them their Calvinist religion and a fierce independence of spirit. Their first and largest settlement is Rehoboth, south of Windhoek.

The Tswana are the smallest of Namibia's ethno-linguistic groups, a number of them occupying a segment of sandveld country bordering southwestern Botswana. They number just 7 000, and are related to the Tswana of the latter country.

THE TOWNS

Windhoek, the capital city, lies 1 680 metres above sea level in semi-arid country 650 kilometres north of the Orange River and 360 kilometres from the Atlantic seaboard - that is to say, almost at the country's geographical epicentre. It has a population of some 150 000, a quarter of whom are citizens of European origin, many of them German-speaking. Its biggest suburb is the sprawling, high-density township of Katutura on the outskirts to the northwest.

Before the coming of the white settlers in the early 1890s the area was occupied

Mounted troops ride down early Windhoek's main thoroughfare in celebration of the Kaiser's birthday.

by Herero and Nama communities, who called the area Aigams ('fire waters') for the number of warm mineral springs, welcome features of an otherwise parched-looking countryside. Despite its arid appearance, though, the land is generous enough, sustaining cattle and karakul sheep, whose pelts are commercially known as Swakara. Welcome, too, is the ring of hills that encircles the city and serves as a barrier against the worst of the drying desert winds.

The German influence is discernible everywhere, and especially in the city's architecture. The first whites built a fort (commonly called the 'Alte Feste' or Old Fort, now part of the State Museum) on a height commanding the settlement, and went on to erect a number of other imposing edifices, among them the Tintenpalast (the administrative centre built in 1913; the nickname means 'palace of ink'); the Christuskirche (1910); the Turnhalle (Gymnasium; 1913); the Genossenschaftshaus (1910) and the adjoining Geschäftshaus Gathemann in Kaiser Street, and three grand German-style castles, namely Schwerinsburg, Sanderburg and Heinitzburg (the first two are now private residences, while the last has been converted into an arts centre).

There is a lot that is still German, too, about the city's social life, or at least that of its colonially descended residents, many of whom observe the customs and speak the language of their land of origin. A major event on the social calendar is the traditional German-style carnival which takes place in Windhoek and other major centres each year. Prime ingredients of this carnival are oompah music and the superb beer that is brewed locally.

Other pleasant attractions are the nearby Daan Viljoen game park (antelope, furnished rondavels, restaurant, swimming pool), the karakul wool carpets woven at Dorka and Dordabis to the east, the picturesque German fort on the farm Klein-Naus and, in Windhoek itself, the superb German delicatessens and bakeries and the locally produced, and quite delicious, Springer chocolates.

But Windhoek is increasingly becoming

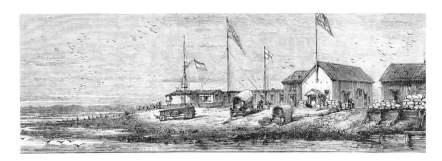

an African city. There is a new generation at the helm, its presence evident in the offices of government, industry and commerce. The streets are thronged with people of a dozen local cultures, the air vibrant with their dialects, and everywhere there is a vitality born of a sense of freedom and pride in self.

The coastal towns

Namibia's long coastline is, if not featureless, remarkably free of promontories, embayments and natural harbours. This, together with the formidably hostile nature of the desert hinterland, has discouraged development. In fact there are only four urban centres of any significance within the entire 1 495-kilometre coastal belt, and one of these owes its existence not to any maritime relevance, but to the wealth that lies in, and sometimes on, the arid, exposed ground. Following a south-to-north sequence, they are:

Oranjemund, a short distance inland and some eight kilometres north of the Orange River mouth, was founded in 1936 to replace Kolmanskop (now a ghost town;) as headquarters of the Namibian diamond industry. A meticulously planned 'company town', home of the Consolidated Diamond Mines (CDM) corporation and one of the world's leading diamond-producing centres, Oranjemund lies within the Sperrgebiet, or restricted area, and one may only enter with permission. The place is maintained by the mine management (there is no civic authority, no private residential ownership) and social and recreational amenities are quite excellent, as, surprisingly, is the climate: the air here is cooled by a kindly wind from the southwest. One is surprised, too, by the amount of greenery that graces the

The first colonial presence: Walvis Bay soon after its annexation by the British in 1878.

streets, parks and neat suburban gardens – a floral richness nurtured by the waters of the Orange. The same source sustains an extensive and efficiently run company farm that supplies the town with fresh meat, dairy products, vegetables and fruit. There is a direct air service from Oranjemund to Windhoek.

Lüderitz, some 270 kilometres up the coast, hugs the shores of a beautifully sheltered embayment which its first European visitor, the Portuguese navigator Bartholemeu Dias, initially named Angra dos Ilheos ('bay of islands'), but shortly thereafter changed it to Angra Pequena ('small bay'). Set between sea and desolate hinterland and far removed from the established centres, the place was more or less ignored by maritime and commercial interests until the 1860s, when Adolf Lüderitz, a German merchant intent on expanding his trading operations (and on some amateur empire-building), persuaded Chancellor Otto von Bismarck to bring the area under German protection, a move that led directly to the colonization of the entire territory.

Later, after diamonds were discovered in the Namib, Lüderitz became a thriving mining village within the Sperrgebiet (unlike Oranjemund, the town itself is open). Today it continues to serve the diggings but is also a busy little centre of the fishing industry (mainly pilchards and rock lobster). Among the town's attractions are its colonial-style buildings, its museum (notable for the Khoisan exhibits), Dias Point, where there is a replica of the *padrão*, or cross, erected by Dias, and the splendid bird life that flourishes on and around the bay. Halifax Island, near Dias Point, is a penguin sanctuary. More than 50 species of succulent can be found in the desert area as well as some fine gemstones.

Walvis Bay, the region's principal port, is within a 1 124-square-kilometre enclave that, at the time of writing, legally belonged to South Africa, though ownership is in dispute. The town, which has a population of some 30 000, lies on the edge of the Namib desert just north of the sporadically flowing Kuiseb River. The bay itself is wide and deep, the anchorage well protected by the Pelican Point peninsula in the northwest. Until recently fishing and fish-processing were the principal local activities (during the 1970s the town boasted ten whitefish and pilchard factories) but over-exploitation of marine resources by foreign as well as Namibian and South African fleets have led to a serious, though probably temporary, decline within the industry. The port, though, is well used and among other things it functions as the major outlet for Namibia's substantial uranium exports.

The Walvis Bay area is something of an ornithologist's paradise. The lagoon to the south of the town is famed for its waterbirds. Nearly 80 different species, among them Pelicans, Damara Terns and migrant Arctic Terns are common there, and at times up to 20 000 flamingoes can be seen feeding in the shallow waters. Just to the east is another sanctuary, a place of reeds and still waters that is home to both marine and freshwater species. Bird Island, north of Walvis Bay, hosts tens of thousands of seabirds that deposit over 900 tons of guano each year on the 1 500-square-metre platform erected during the 1930s.

Some 50 kilometres south of Walvis Bay is Sandwich Harbour, once used by whalers and trading vessels but eventually abandoned, the buildings relinquished to the relentlessly shifting sands of the desert. Fresh water finds its way under the dunes to form pools which, together with the lagoon's seawater, provides an unusual, even unique, environment and here, too, the bird life is prolific (at times

Angra Pequena, later known as Lüderitz Bay, in the days of the sailing ships.

more than half a million individuals congregate in this area) and fascinating. In all about 120 species have been recorded in the vicinity, many of them migrants.

The shores of Sandwich Harbour may well offer other, quite different riches. Just over two centuries ago a sailing ship laden with gold and ivory and precious stones – gifts the Great Mogul of Delhi intended to bestow on Robert Clive (conquerer of India) and valued at the time at a prodigious six million British pounds – came to grief on its way to England, dispersing its fabulous cargo among the ever-changing dunes. There it remains, a perennial challenge to the patience and ingenuity of the treasure-hunter.

Swakopmund, 32 kilometres north of Walvis Bay, is a residential town of some 25 000 people, and the country's foremost seaside resort. The place is surrounded by desert sands that are sometimes whipped to a frenzy by the strong easterly wind, and the waters of the ocean tend to be too chilly for comfortable bathing, but for the rest it's a pleasant enough venue for the tourist and leisure-bent holiday-maker. It has inviting restaurants (Café Anton is a must) and shops, a fine beach, an Olympic-sized, heated pool near the waterfront, and a sheltered swimming area. The sea provides good sport for the surfer and surf-fisherman, and the nearby salt pans are enlivened by myriad coastal and aquatic

birds. Other attractions include an 18-hole golf course, and an excellent museum which features natural history (dioramas of marine and desert life), local history, and marine and mineral displays. The town is graced by some intriguing early-20th-century colonial architecture. Notable buildings include the grandly elaborate railway station (built in 1901), the Woermann House library and art complex (1905), the Kaserne (1905), the prison (1907), and the old magistrate's court.

Local industries include brewing (the Hansa plant is located in town) and the manufacture of durable, and most comfortable, kudu-leather footwear.

Swakopmund is a convenient base from which to explore a countryside full of interest. Close by are the Rössing Mountains and the Rössing uranium mine, the Cape Cross seal colony, the valley of the Swakop River, the desert and in particular the Namib-Naukluft park, which lies to the southeast. Farther afield, to the north, is a fisherman's paradise along the rugged magnificence of the Skeleton Coast.

The inland towns
The main south-north highway through the central uplands connects South Africa's Namaqualand region with Windhoek and the northern Namibian towns of

Ships crowd the waters off Swakopmund during the early years of this century.

Grootfontein, Tsumeb and Oshakati, near the Angolan border. Subsidiary roads branch off to the west and east, leading to other inland centres, most of them tiny, isolated and remarkable only for the sociability of their residents and the hospitality they lavish on visitors. Distances are immense, the terrain often monotonous, the heat and dust constant discomforts – motoring can therefore be a wearisome business, but there is something magical about the great Namibian interior, a quality that seduces the senses, lifts the spirit, and lives in the memory long after the journey is done.

Keetmanshoop, 482 kilometres south of Windhoek, began life as a mission station, established in 1866 to serve the needs of the local Nama, later (in 1894) becoming a German garrison town. The military-colonial past is reflected in the style of some of its larger buildings, prominent among which are the railway station and the fort-like structure that now houses the government offices and police station. The summer climate here is hot, the rainfall low and the sandveld terrain mostly arid, though it supports great numbers of karakul sheep, the mainstay of the local economy. Water supplies are drawn from the Naute Dam on the Löwen River, some 50 kilometres distant and one of

Namibia's largest reservoirs.

Close to town is the Gariganus nature reserve in which a host of primeval quiver-trees or kokerbome grow. Rising starkly from the desert plain to the northwest is the volcanic Brukkaros mountain, the crater of which is a very impressive 2 000 metres in diameter.

Mariental, 221 kilometres farther north, is also a centre of the karakul industry, though the countryside here is rather less harsh (the area is the meeting place of the Kalahari sandveld and the rocky hardveld plain). The principal attraction is the Hardap Dam, 24 kilometres away and centre-piece of a pleasant recreation resort (bungalows, camping and caravanning, a restaurant set spectacularly on a high hill, and angling for yellowfish, mullet and blue kurper) and nature reserve. The latter, 25 000 hectares in extent, is a haven for a wide range of buck and zebra and for more than 100 bird species, including African Fish Eagles and flocks of White-breasted Cormorants. The Hardap Dam, Namibia's first and largest earth-fill reservoir, is fed by the Fish River, and its waters nourish the citrus fruits and vegetables that are cultivated on the floodplain below the 39-metre-high dam wall.

Far to the west of Mariental, incongruously sited on the fringes of the Namib desert southwest of Maltahöhe, is Schloss Duwisib, a German-style castle built in 1908, and sumptuously furnished and

decorated by Baron von Wolff with antiques, works of art and firearms. The castle has been renovated and developed as a tourist attraction.

Rehoboth is a small and refreshingly shady little settlement on the long, sun-baked road from Keetmanshoop to Windhoek. It has been the home of a closely integrated Baster community since 1870.

Gobabis, 205 kilometres to the east of Windhoek, is a railhead and centre of a prosperous ranching industry that extends across the border (120 kilometres distant) into Botswana cattle country. The district is some 10 million hectares in extent and supports 880 farms. Dairy and beef processing plants have been established in town. The name means 'drinking place of elephants', a reference to the nearby Swart-Nossob River.

Okahandja, traditional home of the Herero people, lies astride the Okahandja River and on the main highway 71 kilometres north of Windhoek, serving as a road and rail centre for traffic between the city and Walvis Bay. It also boasts a small airfield. The Hereros moved into the area around 1800, to be followed by the inevitable missionaries: Heinrich Schmelen arrived in 1827 and the Rhenish Society built a church here in 1876.

In August each year thousands of Herero, the women clad in their spectacular 'traditional' costumes, gather in town to pay homage to their dead chiefs, most of whom are buried in the area.

Near Okahandja are two of Namibia's most popular resorts. The Von Bach Dam (watersports, angling, bird-watching, caravan and camping sites) lies a little way to the southeast. Westwards, 26 kilometres along a tarred road, are the Gross Barmen hot springs, a complex of bungalows, restaurant, shop and two mineral pools – the outdoor one attractively palm-fringed, the indoor spacious and well-appointed.

Karibib and Usakos are two lively little villages on the road that leads west to Swakopmund on the coast. A feature of the former is its marble (argonite) industry, of the latter its place in local railway history – the Otavi Mining and Railway

Company narrow-gauge line ran through the area.

Among the tourist drawcards in the general vicinity are the volcanic Erongo mountain range, the western peaks of which rise 2 300 metres above sea level, the fifty or so rock faces near the pleasant Etemba guest farm used by the ancient San artists as their 'canvas', and the splendidly isolated, 1 759-metre Spitzkoppe massif on and around which are some fine galleries of rock paintings (at Rhino Wall, Bushman's Paradise and other sites).

Omaruru, north of Karibib, is a peaceful, attractively embowered place that functions as the centre for the surrounding dairy farms and cattle ranches.

Not too far out of town is the Paula Cave, renowned for its rich variety of rock art. Farther north on the road to Otjiwarongo lies the village of Kalkfeld, gateway to the Etjo Mountain where, 175 million years ago, dinosaurs trod the primeval land. Some of their footprints have been perfectly preserved in a 25-metre stretch of sandstone terrain.

Otjiwarongo, 74 kilometres to the northeast, is a fairly substantial town by Namibia's modest standards. It has a railway station, an airfield, a recreation park, some fine shade trees and a population of around 10 000. It serves a flourishing farming community.

To the south are the twin peaks of the Omatako Mountains (the name means 'buttocks' in the Herero language); the road to the east leads to the 40 000-hectare Waterberg Plateau park.

Outjo, north-west of Otjiwarongo, is the terminus of the branch railway line and a pleasant enough stopover for visitors on their way to the splendid Etosha National Park. The town has a municipal resort (bungalows) and caravan park. Features of the general area include the Ugab Valley terraces, the 'Stone Finger' formation and the volcanic tiger's eye deposits on the farm Hopewell.

Much farther to the west are the village of Khorixas, (beyond which is a spectacular 'petrified forest' of giant and ancient tree-trunks, some of them 30 metres in length and six metres in circumference), the remarkable rock engravings near the hamlet of Kamanjab, Twyfelfontein ('fountain of doubt') and the Burnt Mountain, a strange place of sun-baked, multi-hued rock formations. At Twyfelfontein, among a moonscape of jumbled outcrops and boulders, is one of the country's most extensive rock-art collections. The engravings, some of them dating back 5 000 years, are thought to be the work of ancestral Khoi while the paintings are of Bushman origin.

Otavi lies in a pleasantly wooded and fertile plain beneath the towering (2 148 metres) Otavi Mountains. The name is derived from the Herero word *ondavi* meaning 'branch of a tree'. Otavi is attractively tree-shaded, and functions as a copper-mining and farming centre.

Grootfontein, due east of Otavi, is a fair-sized town, notable for its flowering trees (including jacarandas, which reach their lilac-coloured glory in September), its German fort, built in 1897 and now a museum, its fountain, exotic Tree Park, and the 60-ton Hoba meteorite 20 kilometres to the west, discovered in 1920 and, so far as is known, the largest in existence. It is composed largely of nickel and lead.

The wandering Thirstland (or Dorsland) Boer trekkers, who set off from the Pretoria and Rustenburg districts in the 1870s to make their way across the arid wastes of northern Botswana and into Angola, briefly settled in the Grootfontein area in the 1880s and attempted to establish a miniscule 'Republic of Upingtonia' before returning north. (Their descendants remained in Angola until the 1920s, when they were resettled in Namibia.) Today Grootfontein serves as a shipping point for timber from the Kavango region 250 kilometres to the northeast. Other local industries process meat and dairy products and leather goods, and copper and lead are mined in the region to the west and transported to Tsumeb for smelting.

Tsumeb, 426 kilometres north of Windhoek and the terminus of the main south-north railway (a line also leads to Swakopmund) is a pleasant 'company town' and the centre of a vigorous mining industry. The name is a corruption of the local word *sumeb*, which describes the moss-green appearance of the almost pure copper ore-body outcrop, and it aptly reflects the area's mineral wealth. The region was originally home to Damara and San groups, but long before the colonial era visiting Wambo peoples worked the deposits, fashioning the copper into jewellery and utensils.

The Tsumeb mine, based on a giant 'pipe' that reaches fully 1 500 metres beneath the surface, is famed for the fact that more than 200 minerals are found there. Among these are lead, silver, zinc, cadmium, germanium and arsenic, apart from the copper. Less valuable but exquisite to behold are the crystallized oxidic deposits – azurite, malachite, dioptase and so forth – that are mined here and eventually find their way onto collectors' shelves the world over.

Tsumeb is an attractively laid-out town, its streets and gardens decorated with flowering trees and shrubs. Some 20 kilometres to the north is the Otjikoto sunken lake, in which there are great numbers of fish, some of which belong to rare, even unique species. It is thought that their remote ancestors were stranded here by retreating floodwaters, leaving succeeding generations to follow their own evolutionary paths. Most unusual of all are the two types of fish that hatch the fertilized eggs in their mouths. A sister lake, Guinas, lies some 20 kilometres distant.

Oshakati, largest of the Wambo settlements in this generally densely populated northern region, is 290 kilometres from Tsumeb. The countryside here is flat, sandy, sparsely grassed for the most part but thickly wooded with acacia and mopane trees in patches, and criss-crossed by shallow watercourses called *oshanas*. The rural economy is based on stock-farming, the cultivation of maize and *muhango* (millet), melons, beans, pumpkins and, to a somewhat lesser extent, on fish caught in the *oshanas*.

Oshakati is an important light industrial and commercial centre, well geared to supply a variety of goods to the region's nearly 10 000 small 'cuca' outlets (the name derives from the excellent Angolan beer that was sold through the shops before the insurgency war).

Near Oshakati is the educational centre of Ongwandiva and to the west, on the Angolan border, is Ruacana, site of a massive hydro-electric project launched in the 1970s. The Ruacana Falls on the Kunene River are one of the country's most splendid natural wonders.

THE WILDERNESS

Pride of Namibia and one of Africa's finest game sanctuaries is the Etosha, a 23 000-square-kilometre national park centred on a pan, or shallow depression, that measures an impressive 130 by 50 kilometres.

One of the interpretations of the name 'Etosha' is 'place of mirages', a piece of imagery that captures the essence of the pan. Its origins are something of a mystery, but millennia ago it was probably a huge lake fed by the waters of the Kunene before that river, at some point in the distant past, changed its course. The lake dried out, leaving a briny, mineral-rich plain – a 'salt desert' incapable of sustaining plant life. However, the saline and mineral residues and the moisture from the summer rains and the overflow of rivers attract immense numbers of game.

The moisture begins to disappear from about March, leaving a strange winterscape of hard, dazzlingly white flatland where the air shimmers in the heat, and it is during these months that the 'mirages' are at their most striking. Around the pan, and elsewhere in the park, the terrain is more hospitable, much of it covered by sweet grasses, deciduous trees and mopane and acacia woodlands.

Etosha is home to about 1 500 elephant, as well as rhino, lion, leopard, cheetah, 7 000 zebra, 2 600 blue wildebeest, 20 000 springbok, kudu, hartebeest, eland, the unusual black impala, the endearing Damara dik-dik (one of the smallest of the antelope) and other buck

species. The bird life, too, is remarkably rich: to date, 325 species have been recorded – some of them rare – ranging in size from the miniscule prinia to the stately ostrich. When the rains fall, flamingoes and pelicans arrive in thousands.

This magnificent array of wildlife is best seen at the permanent waterholes, most of which are in the park's central and eastern regions.

There are three rest-camps at Etosha, pleasantly shady places that offer comfortable bungalows, restaurants and shops. The Namutoni camp also has a museum, housed in a romantic Beau Geste-type fort built by the German military colonists in the early years of the century. The Okaukuejo camp is sited beside a magnificent waterhole which is floodlit by night.

The Namib-Naukluft desert park lies far to the south of Etosha, on the coast around and inland from Walvis Bay. This is a sweeping wasteland of dunes (those around Sossusvlei, rising in places to a full 300 metres, are reputedly the highest in the world), drifting sand and gravel plains, mists that roll in from the sea, solitude and an immense silence.

It is also a place of some vegetation: here (notably on the Welwitschia Flats north of the Swakop River) grows the weird welwitschia, a large, withered-looking species which can live for a thousand years, produces just two leaves in its lifetime, and was termed by the great Charles Darwin 'the platypus of the plant kingdom'. Around the pools of the Kuiseb canyon and the rare waterholes, and along the ancient river beds that flood perhaps two or three times a century but where there is moisture deep underground, patches of euphorbia, camelthorn, wild fig and ana trees relieve the otherwise barren terrain. The water and sparse flora sustain a variety of animals, among them gemsbok, klipspringer, steenbok, springbok, leopard, jackal, and brown and spotted hyaena.

South of the park lies diamond country, a restricted region where fabulous quantities of beautiful and precious stones are recovered from the sands and gravels.

Combined with the Namib-Naukluft, the region forms one of southern Africa's most extensive conservation areas, and the fourth largest in the world.

The Skeleton Coast park, far up the Atlantic seaboard, is a slender (40 kilometres at its widest), 600-kilometre strip of sand and gravel, jagged ravines, dolorite dykes and some of the world's most desolate shores.

The park stretches from the Ugab River in the south to the Kunene and the Angolan border. A road in fairly good condition – it has a hard, salty surface – takes you part of the way northwards, to Torra Bay, where there's a caravan and camping ground, and on to Terrace Bay, which boasts a restaurant, shop and rooms for hire. The more intrepid visitor can explore a corner of this extraordinary region on foot, embarking on the 52-kilometre, three-day Ugab River hiking trail along the park's southern boundary. Others join the five-day safari expedition that starts from a tented camp at Sarusas.

Although the Skeleton Coast may appear wholly barren at first sight, it too has its fauna and flora, radically adapted and often unique to this unforgiving environment. Most of the plant and insect species depend for their moisture on the thick fog that envelops the coast and hinterland, and in the northern edges of the wilderness, where there are rivers of sorts as well as underground water, birds and game animals manage to survive and even flourish. Here are found elephant, black rhino, mountain zebra, giraffe, lion, cheetah and a variety of buck. Jackals have learnt to subsist on what they can glean from the coast's storm-battered beaches.

Cape Cross seal reserve, to the south of the Skeleton Coast park, is a rocky sanctuary for between 80 000 and 100 000 of these marine mammals, and for great flocks of Cape Cormorants.

The Brandberg lies a hundred kilometres inland and just south of the Ugab River. Here the terrain changes dramatically, rising up in an immense massif, or series of massifs, fully 500 square kilometres in extent. The 2 579-metre Königstein is the highest peak in Namibia.

The crags and rocky overhangs of the Brandberg are the location of some of the finest of all San paintings. Some of the art, in fact, is much older than the present San culture, and one piece enjoys special notoriety. This is the so-called White Lady, deep in the wild and lovely Tsisab ('leopard') gorge. This is a pale, attractive figure that the celebrated Abbé Breuil, who visited the site in 1948, believed to have been of Phoenician or other alien origin. The depiction, though, is in truth probably that of a masculine and almost certainly local subject. The White Lady is just one of a whole gallery of splendid paintings to be found in the Maack Cave.

Fish River Canyon park. Slicing through the arid terrain just north of the Orange River is one of the world's most spectacular natural formations, the 161-kilometre-long, and in places 27-kilometre-wide Fish River Canyon, centrepiece of an extensive park which also encloses the mountains to the west. Only Arizona's Grand Canyon is bigger.

The cliffs to either side of this gigantic gash in the countryside fall 500 metres sheer to the valley below. Through this flows the Fish River, one of Namibia's longest watercourses. It rises in the Naukluft hills to the north and meanders 800 kilometres or so before joining its big brother, the Orange, on its way to the Atlantic Ocean. The Fish River's flow is seasonal, though it leaves deep pools that outlast even the longest and driest of winters. The floor of the canyon is distinguished by its immensely ancient rocks – some of the Achaean granites and gneisses are 2 600 million years old – and by its warm mineral springs. Farther downriver the Ai-Ais hot springs mark the site of an attractive little resort. The waters of Ai-Ais emerge at a constant 60 °C.

Air temperatures here are high too, becoming almost unbearably so in the depths of the valley, and indeed Ai-Ais is closed to visitors during the blistering summer months. Winters are cooler, and it is then that the more adventurous among the hiking fraternity challenge the terrain, setting off on the 86-kilometre Fish River Canyon trail through a land-scape weathered to starkness by water and the sand-blasting wind. A far less demanding exploratory route is the road that leads 60 kilometres along the eastern side of the gorge. There are digressions to viewsites from which the vistas are quite breathtaking, especially at sunrise and sunset, and paths wind down to the banks of the river below.

The northeastern reserves. Three significant conservation areas sprawl across the sandveld and scrub of the far northeastern corner of the country. None of them is well developed at present, though all have excellent tourism potential.

The Caprivi game park is a rugged expanse of densely wooded country that

Jan Jonker Afrikaner, warlike leader of the Nama in the troubled 19th century.

serves as sanctuary for elephant and buffalo and a number of buck, including the rare roan antelope.

Along Caprivi's southwestern boundary with Botswana is the 25 000-hectare Mahango game reserve, an ecologically diverse area of grasslands, flood plains, riverine forests and reed and papyrus beds, all of which elements combine to sustain over 60 species of mammal – the big cats, elephant, hippo, kudu, sable, roan antelope and such lesser known buck as the lechwe, the oribi and the shy sitatunga.

Even newer is the Kaudom game reserve (300 000 hectares), a rugged, rather featureless stretch of dry wooded sandveld accessible only to four-wheel-drive vehicles that supports a remarkable number and variety of animals. They are most prolific when the rains enrich the grassland spaces.

Waterberg Plateau park, in north-central Namibia and east of Otjiwarongo, is a 40 000-hectare woodland and savanna sanctuary for white rhino, buffalo, roan, sable, eland and other antelope.

The plateau itself, a place of rugged sandstone formations and precipitous cliffs, rises imposingly above the plains. A remnant of the original crust that has gained prominence by the erosion of the surrounding countryside, it is 48 kilometres long and eight to 10 kilometres wide, and its southern foothills are graced by life-sustaining, free-flowing springs around which large trees (among them wild figs) grow and within which a number of frog species have evolved independently. Some of the plant life is also unique to the area. Travel within the park is restricted, largely to preserve its untamed character and its rare species. There are no roads, but hides and viewpoints are accessible to walkers. The Waterberg guided wilderness trail (15 kilometres a day for four days) follows a circular route around the western slopes; the park's accommodation comprises two trail camps and, for the less energetic visitor, a recently established rest camp (chalets, campsites, shop, restaurant, swimming pool).

Mount Etjo safari lodge, in north-central Namibia (250 kilometres north of Windhoek), is one of southern Africa's more luxuriously attractive guest farms, blessed with a generous number of dams and waterholes, and a fine profusion of wildlife on its grassland spaces. Much of it, such as the elephant, white rhino and antelope, was reintroduced in recent years.

Mount Etjo is only one of a growing number of private game lodges and guest farms that contribute significantly both to the conservation of Namibia's priceless wildlife heritage and to the country's expanding tourist industry.

THE PAST

Namibia became a geographically defined entity only towards the end of the 19th century, when the European colonial powers – Britain, Germany and Portugal – negotiated the boundary settlements that established German South West Africa.

Long before then, though, the semi-arid highlands and the deserts had been infiltrated and often fought over by groups of Khoisan and Bantu-speaking peoples.

First to arrive in force were the San hunter-gatherers, who roamed the great sunlit spaces a thousand and more years before the birth of Christ and who adorned the caves and rock shelters of the north-central uplands with their marvellously animated paintings. Much later these gentle folk came into contact and conflict with the Nama pastoralists, descendants of the Khoikhoi (Hottentots) of the Cape Province in South Africa who had occupied the Orange River region and who, from the early 18th century, began moving northwards into the arid Namibian interior.

By this time both the Bergdama and the Wambo had appeared on the scene, the latter migrating from Central Africa to settle the northern flatlands around the Kunene River. They were followed, in the late 18th century, by the Herero, who penetrated into the Kaokoveld in the northwest and down into the midlands, and from the south by bands of Oorlams, an aggressive, unruly people of largely mixed Khoikhoi-slave ancestry who had adopted European ways and came armed with European weapons.

The vanguard of the powerful Oorlams trekker-marauders was led by one Jager Afrikaner, a man of some military talent but also of mixed loyalties: he had helped the Cape Dutch government in its campaign to contain the San raiders of the colonial border areas, but later turned to banditry, retreating far beyond the Orange when a punitive expedition was dispatched from Cape Town. Well-armed and safely ensconced in Namaland, he continued his plundering ways until his eventual conversion to Christianity, after which he lived peaceably enough until his death in 1823. However, his successors, Jonker and Jan Jonker Afrikaner, were to play significant roles in the vicious inter-group rivalries of the 19th century.

The last of the pre-colonial immigrants were the Basters, also of mixed (mainly Dutch-Nama) descent and a Calvinistic, fiercely independent people. Boer settler pressure drove some of the Baster communities north of the Orange in the late 1860s, to an area south of today's Windhoek, where they established a settlement that became known as Rehoboth.

The middle decades of the 19th century were troubled years: competition for

Heinrich Schmelen, founder of the German evangelical mission in 1815.

water and grazing lands, for territory, for supremacy between the various peoples and, in particular, between the Nama and the Herero, led to open, merciless and generally inconclusive warfare during the 1840s, throughout the 1860s, and again in the 1880s.

The coming of the Europeans

Portuguese navigators, seeking the sea route to the Indies, began charting the Namibian coastline in the closing years of the 15th century, dropping anchor at Cape Cross, Walvis Bay and Dias Point, and small areas of the hinterland were tentatively explored by succeeding generations of Dutch, English and French mariners. But for over 300 years the nation states of Europe gave little thought to establishing a permanent presence as the endless, empty wastes were simply too forbidding.

The sea and the offshore islands, though, did attract a sizeable number of European entrepreneurs and were commercially exploited long before the colonial era, the former by 18th-century American and British whaling and sealing fleets, the latter after the discovery of rich deposits of guano (nitrogen-rich sea-bird droppings) in 1843. Indeed, at the peak of the great mid-century 'guano rush' little Ichaboe Island, which lies to the north of Lüderitz Bay, played host to fully 400 sailing ships and a motley workforce of 6 000 sailors and labourers.

There was also a modicum of activity on the political front during the pre-colonial decades. In 1793 the Dutch government at the Cape placed Walvis Bay, Lüderitz Bay and other coastal areas under Dutch protection, a move designed to forestall foreign territorial and commercial competition. Two years later the British occupied the Cape of Good Hope and inherited the 'protectorates', though formal proprietorship was delayed for almost a century. The Guano Islands were annexed to the Crown in 1867 and the territory of Walvis Bay in 1878. Walvis Bay and the islands became the property of the Cape colonial government in 1884.

Spreading the Word

A trickle of explorers, cattle-traders, Boer trekkers and prospectors (after the discovery of copper in the south) filtered into the territory during the 19th century. Among the trailblazers was the noted elephant hunter Jacobus Coetse who crossed the Orange in 1760, followed by Hendrik Hop, who reached the vicinity of present-day Keetmanshoop, and Pieter Brand, who travelled as far as the Aus Mountains and the Swakop River. In 1793 Pieter Pienaar anchored in Walvis Bay and penetrated far inland by following the course of the Swakop River.

A detachment of the Schutztruppe camel corps about to set out on desert patrol.

It was the men of God, however, who launched the first concerted white assault on the great interior. The earliest of the missionaries, Abraham and Christian Albrecht, settled among the Nama in the early 1800s, and Heinrich Schmelen founded the Bethanien mission station in 1815, so establishing a German evangelical presence that heralded, and prepared the ground for the seminal arrival of the Rhenish Mission Society in 1842.

Before the end of the decade the newcomers were teaching and preaching to Jan Jonker Afrikaner's people around Windhoek, at Walvis Bay and Rehoboth and at Otjimbingwe on the Swakop River. Later, stations were founded farther afield, most successfully among the Nama, part of whose cultural origins lay in the Calvinism of the Dutch-ruled Cape. The Hereros, of tenaciously independent disposition and proud of their traditions, were a great deal more resistant to the Christian message.

In 1870 Lutheran pastors of the Finnish Missionary Society settled among the Wambo of the far north .

The colonial impetus

The ethnic wars of the latter part of the century, and the widespread havoc these wreaked, prompted repeated requests from missionaries, from white (mostly German) traders and from a German government who felt some responsibility for their welfare for British imperial involvement. These were routinely rejected until 1876, when the Cape authorities concluded a series of treaties with local leaders that technically extended the Cape colonial administration's authority beyond the Orange. Two years later Britain agreed to annex Walvis Bay.

Neither of these moves, though, brought any degree of stability to the war-torn land as the British had no intention of becoming embroiled in tribal quarrels and Cape politicians were preoccupied with troubles elsewhere on the subcontinent (notably in the eastern Cape border and Basutoland regions), and it was finally left to the German authorities, in the person of Chancellor von Bismarck, to grasp the initiative.

This he did in 1884, when Adolf Lüderitz, a Hamburg trader operating from the bay that was shortly to bear his name, petitioned the German leadership for protection. The response was immediate and favourable, developing within a very short time into full-scale annexation of the entire territory we now know as Namibia. Excluded were the Walvis Bay enclave and the islands, which Britain retained.

Rebellion and reprisal

During the first few colonial years the machinery of government remained simple, even rudimentary: the formal administration in Windhoek comprised little more than the Imperial Commissioner, his secretary and a few officials. Outside the 'capital', Otjimbingwe, effective control lay largely with the mercantile and mining companies which were vested with a degree of legal and military authority.

Later, the German state assumed greater responsibility for running the young protectorate, and for keeping civil order in a territory that had been at war with itself for over half a century. In 1889 Captain Curt von Francois and a platoon of 23 men were dispatched from Walvis Bay with instructions to restrict the supply of arms and ammunition to the fighting factions and to restore peace to the countryside, and over the following months and years the Germans gradually extended their military capability. In May 1894 the purely protective role assigned to the armed forces was abandoned and the contingents became Imperial *Schutztruppe*. Several stone forts were erected and various minor rebellions quelled.

Meanwhile, the colonial community had grown in size. Traders and merchant companies were making healthy profits, white farmers (the first had arrived in 1892) were settling more and more of the grasslands, roads had been built and railways planned, and the territory was making modest but fairly steady progress on the economic front.

All of this seemed satisfactory enough in the context of imperial aspiration, but to the Herero and Nama the 'progress' represented a direct threat to traditional freedoms and therefore a challenge to be confronted. The former in particular bitterly resented white encroachment and all that it brought in the form of alien laws and levies, the expropriation of land and the erosion of age-old rights to common pastures and water resources. Towards the end of 1903 the Nama rose in revolt, drawing most of the *Schutztruppe* to the south. A few months later the Herero, temporarily relieved of their watchdogs, also took up arms against the colonial regime and in so doing began one of the most horrific chapters in the annals of the territory.

The Herero rebellion lasted almost four years, led to the loss of many German lives (though, significantly, Boer and English settlers were not molested) and in the end, after 88 bloody engagements, to the extermination of three-quarters of the Herero nation. By 1907 these proud people, 80 000 strong at the beginning of hostilities, were reduced to a handful of starving refugees.

Some 65 000 Herero died during these brutal years, most of them of hunger and thirst in the barren desert wastes of the east. The descendants of the 15 000 survivors were eventually resettled in the almost equally inhospitable sandveld region of present-day Hereroland.

The desert treasure-house

The existence of large diamond deposits along Namibia's barren coastline had been suspected as early as 1863, when a Cape Town enterprise negotiated with the local chief a concession to explore a 30-kilometre strip north of the Orange River. Nothing was found, though – until half a century later.

In 1908 an ex-Kimberley labourer, Zacharias Lewala, recognized the glitter of diamonds in the sand he was shovelling near the railway line at Grasplatz, a tiny railway siding just to the east of Lüderitz. The news spread, prospectors converged on the area, and within a few months thousands of hectares had been pegged.

The mining world of the day tended to discount the discoveries – in fact the secretary of the giant De Beers conglomerate reported the deposits to be 'greatly over-exaggerated', and experts predicted a maximum recovery of 1,5 million carats from the fields.

Nevertheless, the German authorities declared the land 'forbidden territory' or *Sperrgebiet* and awarded the Deutsche Diamanten Gesellschaft the sole prospecting rights. In 1920, five years after South African forces occupied German South West Africa, the concession was transferred to Consolidated Diamond Mines, which amalgamated the various workings, now concentrated between Lüderitz and Bogenfels.

The hospital at Kolmanskop, the once-thriving diamond settlement that is now a ghost town.

By this time it was quite clear that the experts who had forecast such low returns had grossly undervalued the fields. They were, and still are, immensely rich. In 1987 alone output was pegged at 1 019 636 carats.

The town that died. One especially evocative relic of the early diamond days is Kolmanskop, site of the first find. The rush prompted by the discovery led to the establishment of a busy little village served by a general dealer, butchery, bakery, furniture factory, soda-water and lemonade plant, daily ice and milk deliveries, four skittle alleys, a public playground and swimming pool, a grand community centre complete with a theatre and an orchestra that played at tea dances, and a well-equipped hospital that housed the country's first X-ray machine (and, charmingly, a wine cellar). Splendid houses were built for the mining executives of the Deutsche Diamanten Gesellschaft.

But the diamond deposits in the immediate vicinity became depleted, and the townspeople began to move away to fresher fields around the new towns of

German settlers take action against the Herero during the wars fought between 1904 and 1907.

Oranjemund (established in 1936) and farther south in Namaqualand.

Finally abandoned, Kolmanskop became a ghost town, a sad place of sagging buildings, peeling paint and silent streets buried by the shifting desert sands. Later there were efforts to restore the village, and to preserve it as a tourist attraction.

South African mandate

South West Africa (SWA) was the first German possession to fall to the Western Allies during the Great War of 1914-18. General Louis Botha, prime minister of the Union of South Africa, and his lieutenant, General Jan Smuts (both loyal 'Empire men'), had to contend with a full-scale Boer rebellion at home before they could marshal their forces for the planned invasion of their country's northwestern neighbour. But the uprising, serious though it might have been, was swiftly crushed, and by February 1915 the two generals were able to take the field, Botha's 12 000-man army landing at Swakopmund and Smuts's 6 000 troops at Lüderitz Bay. Other Union forces marched in from the Orange River.

The *Schutztruppe* were vastly outnumbered and the invaders' chief enemies turned out to be the heat and hostile terrain, as well as the mines and poisoned wells the retreating Germans left behind them. Yet by May 1915 the campaign had been brought to a conclusion and an interim South African military administration was installed in Windhoek.

In terms of the 1919 Treaty of Versailles the German Empire renounced rights to all its colonial possessions in favour of the Allies, and in December of the following year the League of Nations entrusted South West Africa to the Union of South Africa as a 'C' mandate. The agreement, signed in Geneva, gave the Union powers to administer the former colony as an integral part of South Africa subject to certain guarantees, which included, among other things, the economic and social advancement of the local inhabitants but not – and this was the significant ommission – advancement towards self-government.

Neverthless, two constitutional adjustments were made in the mid-1920s: South Africa conferred a degree of independence on the Rehoboth Baster community following their rebellion in 1924, and a year later the territory's whites were granted their own Legislative Assembly. The great majority of Namibians, though, continued to be excluded from the democratic process.

In 1946, the United Nations trusteeship replaced the League's mandate, but South Africa rejected the handing over of the territory and decided that South West Africa should in future be regarded as the Union's 'fifth province'.

Accordingly, in 1949, SWA's whites were invited to vote their own representatives to the South African parliament, and all reference to the UN mandate was deleted from the territory's constitution. As it turned out this was somewhat premature, because shortly thereafter the International Court of Justice at The Hague ruled that the original mandate was in fact still valid.

Four years later the United Nations established its Committee on South West Africa, a body charged with 'supervising' the mandate, and then, in 1956, its General Assembly voted to negotiate an end to Pretoria's control of the territory. The pattern of future confrontation, of the protracted interplay of diplomatic pressure and counter-move, had been set.

The seeds of rebellion

Popular resistance to South Africa's authority in SWA – arguably a 'legal' authority but one which was progressively abused after the watershed National Party victory at the 1948 polls – began in a small way in the latter half of the 1950s with the formation of the Ovamboland People's Congress (OPC) in Cape Town, a body that was renamed the Ovamboland People's Organization in 1959.

In 1960 this body became the South West African People's Organization (Swapo), an as yet non-violent pressure group led by Shafiishuna Samuel Nujoma and Adimba Herman Toivo ja Toivo.

Political profile. Sam Nujoma, destined to become first president of an independent Namibia, was born in Ongandjera, Owambo in 1929, receiving his education at the Finnish (Lutheran) mission school in his home area and at St Barnabas school in Windhoek. As a young adult he worked on the State railways in Cape Town (where he first met ja Toivo) for a number of years before being dismissed for his trade-union activities.

Shortly afterwards he returned to Windhoek where, in 1959, he helped organize opposition to the forced removal of the city's African population from the 'Old

South African officers emerge from Windhoek's Rathaus after the German capitulation in 1915.

Location' to the sprawling Katutura township. Resistance to the removal order led to police action, and to the death of 11 demonstrators. Nujoma was ordered to return to Owambo and in February 1960 he went into exile.

Sponsored by Ghana's Kwame Nkrumah, Nujoma journeyed to the United States to appear before the UN's Committee on South West Africa, and to plan, with Mkurumba Kerina, the reconstitution of the OPC as the South West African People's Organization (Swapo). Kerina became Swapo's first chairman, Nujoma its president.

Nujoma then returned to Africa, establishing Swapo's headquarters in Dar es Salaam, Tanzania.

The long road to independence

The first Swapo cadres to receive guerrilla training travelled to Egypt in 1962, at a time when the organization still hoped for peaceful progress towards majority rule.

In the event, the hope was to diminish rapidly, disappearing altogether in 1966, when the International Court of Justice again upheld South Africa's legal right to govern the territory. The decision was disputed by the UN General Assembly, which formally revoked the mandate.

Thereafter, events moved rapidly. Security forces and insurgents clashed violently at Omgulumubashe on 26 August 1966 (the date became internationally recognized as 'Namibia Day'); Pretoria declared a state of emergency in the territory; and Nujoma committed Swapo – now accepted by the Organization of African Unity (OAU) as a 'national liberation movement' – to the armed struggle.

The following quarter of a century saw progressively intensive diplomatic and military efforts to break South Africa's iron grip on the territory's affairs. The issue, never simple, was complicated even further by Pretoria's attempts to reach an internal accord and, latterly, by the presence of Cuban troops in neighbouring Angola, an element that became intertwined with negotiations for Namibia's independence.

Indeed, the story is so intricate, even labyrinthine, that it is probably best summed up in chronological order:

1967: Toivo ja Toivo and other Swapo internal leaders are tried in Pretoria under the Terrorism Act (proclaimed retroactive for the purposes of the trial), convicted and jailed. Nujoma remains in exile.

1968: Swapo in exile proposes that South West Africa be renamed Namibia.

1969: The UN Security Council declares South Africa's occupation of the territory illegal and calls for unconditional withdrawal. Two years later the World Court reverses its earlier judgments, ruling the occupation illegal.

1972: Local police and security forces crush an uprising in Owambo. Kurt Waldheim, the UN secretary-general, pays a visit to SWA, and in the following year declares Swapo the 'sole and authentic representative' of the Namibian people. Swapo is accorded observer status at the United Nations.

1973: South Africa extends its homelands system, the cornerstone of its 'grand apartheid' design, by agreeing with 'ethnic leaders' to establish the 'self-governing territories' of Ovamboland, Kavango, Caprivi and Rehoboth. There is bloodshed in the streets of Windhoek after rioting breaks out in neighbouring Katutura.

1975: South Africa convenes the Turnhalle constitutional conference to negotiate 'self-government'.

1977: Pretoria dissolves the Turnhalle talks after the formation of the Democratic Turnhalle Alliance (DTA), and appoints an administrator (Mr Justice Steyn) to rule the territory by proclamation.

1978: The UN Security Council passes Resolution 435, which becomes the key to all future international attempts to devise a formula for Namibian independence. South Africa agrees in principle to the Resolution, but rejects the 'Waldheim Plan' for its implementation and, instead, attempts to push through an internal settlement. A 50-seat constituent assembly is created and an election held, which the DTA wins handsomely. Swapo declines to cooperate, and does not contest the election.

Earlier in the year, the South African Defence Force (SADF) raids the Cassinga refugee camp in Angola.

1979: Abortive independence talks are held between Swapo, the Western Five (the United States, Britain, France, West Germany and Canada), the Frontline States (particularly Angola, Zambia, Moçambique, Botswana and later Zimbabwe) and South Africa. Swapo's military wing, Plan, intensifies the armed struggle in Ovambo and Caprivi.

1980: The constitution is amended to accommodate a three-tier government organized on ethnic-group lines; principal features of the arrangement are separate legislative assemblies for the various groups, and a national assembly and council of ministers with limited powers. This 'internal settlement' also creates the South West Africa Territorial Force (SWATF) and the SWA Police Force.

1981: The UN convenes all-party discussions in Geneva, which break down over what South Africa perceives as the UN's pro-Swapo bias. United States President Ronald Reagan links Namibian independence with the withdrawal of Cuban troops from neighbouring Angola.

1982: SA finally endorses Resolution 435 after the UN introduces new clauses.

1983: Pretoria refuses to move towards independence; the internal government resigns; the national assembly is dissolved; the administrator-general resumes office on a caretaker basis.

1984-1986: A Multi-Party Conference (MPC) of six internal political groups (including the DTA and the Swapo-Democrats) is convened to agree a joint policy on Resolution 435. South Africa and Angola hold talks in Lusaka and Angola agrees to the eventual withdrawal of Cuban troops. Herman Toivo ja Toivo is released from prison. In 1985 the MPC asks the President of South Africa, P.W. Botha, for, and is granted, a Transitional Government of National Unity made up of a legislature and an executive authority, and a constitutional council. The latter, chaired by Mr Justice Hiemstra, is charged with producing a lasting constitution, one not based on colour or ethnic group.

1987: The transitional government demonstrates an independent will, and P.W. Botha warns that any steps it takes 'which interferes with South Africa's international interests and undertakings are unacceptable'. The transitional government, in turn, requests South Africa to allow Namibians to 'consider their constitutional future themselves'. There is heavy fighting in the Cuito Cuanavale area of Angola involving Cuban, Angolan, Unita, South African and South West African forces.

1988: The administrator-general is given even wider powers to govern, and in the early part of the year there is doubt concerning South Africa's sincerity in working towards independence. However, in May the first of a series of meetings are held between Angola, Cuba, South Africa and the United States in Brazzaville (Congo), Paris, London, New York, Geneva and elsewhere to negotiate the withdrawal of South African and Cuban troops from Angola. In August, Swapo unilaterally announces a ceasefire in the 22-year-old bush war. In December the Brazzaville Accord is signed by Cuba, Angola and South Africa. In terms of the agreement Cuban troops are to be progressively withdrawn to the northern areas of Angola, and SA forces are to leave Namibia, whose transition to full indepedence is set to begin on 1 April 1989.

1989: Implementation of UN Resoluion 435 begins on 1 April, though Swapo incursions immediately after that date temporarily threaten the process. In September Sam Nujoma returns to Namibia after nearly 30 years in exile. Elections supervised by the United Nations Transitional Assistance Group (Untag) are held on 11 November; Swapo gains a majority of seats in the constituent assembly but not enough to give it complete control. A month later the assembly agrees to adopt a Western-style constitution.

1990: In February, Sam Nujoma is unanimously elected to the office of president by the deputies to the constituent assembly. At midnight on 20 March, at a ceremony in Windhoek, the South African flag is lowered and replaced by the newly designed flag of the Republic of Namibia (comprising diagonal stripes of blue, red and green separated by white lines, with a golden sun at top left). Sam Nujoma is sworn in as the country's first president by UN Secretary-General Javier Perez de Cuellar.

1991: Namibia, the youngest member of the Commonwealth, plays host to Queen Elizabeth II and Prince Philip.

GOVERNMENT

Namibia is a multi-party, unitary republic, its leaders committed to a Western-style democratic arrangement somewhat different from that preferred by Swapo in the pre-independence years, but in keeping with the world-wide move away from authoritarian rule, a trend that gathered momentum after the disintegration of the Soviet empire in the late 1980s. The governmental structures were adopted by the interim constituent assembly, after almost 80 days of careful deliberation, on 9 February 1990.

The constitution places heavy emphasis on the protection of human rights and liberties, and firm restrictions on the powers of the executive. The basic freedoms of thought, speech and the press, of religion and association, are guaranteed by a bill of rights and are 'non-derogable' (that is to say, no government, however well-supported, may remove or dilute them). Expressly outlawed are the death penalty, inhuman treatment, forced labour, and discrimination on the grounds of race, creed, colour, sex and social or economic status.

Also constitutionally enshrined are the rights to own property, to take 'affirmative action' in order to redress imbalances created during the apartheid years, and, on the labour front, to strike.

Detention without trial, a volatile issue in southern Africa, has legal sanction, but only in exceptional circumstances – specifically when either a state of emergency or martial law has been declared.

The constitution also establishes English as the official medium of communication, despite the small number of Namibians who use it as their home language.

The executive. Namibia's head of state is the executive president who is directly elected by the people (he must obtain at least 50 per cent of the votes) for a maximum term of five years, and who may hold office for a maximum of two such terms. He appoints, and carries out the functions of, government with the help of a prime minister and Council of Ministers, or cabinet. Government policy is guided by a set of twelve constitutionally enshrined principles designed 'to promote and maintain the welfare of the people'.

The president is subject to the legislative authority of parliament (see below), which in turn is bound by the provisions of the constitution. He is empowered to declare a state of emergency and thereby to suspend certain laws and restrict certain freedoms, but he must seek the National Assembly's approval for his actions within 30 days of the declaration.

The legislature. The country's constitution makes provision for a two-chamber parliament. The lower chamber comprises a National Assembly of 72 members, elected every five years through a party-list, proportional representation system. In addition, six non-voting members may be appointed by the president.

The upper chamber, the National Council – which had yet to be constituted at the time of writing – will give representation to the various regional councils.

Also envisaged is a Council of Traditional Leaders, a body designed to reflect and reconcile the country's cultural diversity. Its functions will be defined and its powers limited by parliament.

The judiciary. Justice is administered, and the bill of rights guaranteed, by an independent judiciary acting through open courts. These courts may, however – 'for reasons of morals, the public order or national security' – conduct their proceedings behind closed doors. Namibia's highest judicial authority remains the Supreme Court.

Security. The South West Africa Territorial Force (SWATF), which cooperated with the South African military establishment during the war years, was disbanded in

1989, to be replaced by a small, integrated (PLAN/SWATF) permanent unit from which Namibia's 9 000-man, British trained standing army has been developed.

The Namibian Police (Nampol) is also an integrated force, trained by British and Canadian instructors. It comprises elements of both Swapo and the pre-independence, para-military South West Africa Police (Swapol), whose leadership and structure were retained. The new government's stated aims were to 'civilianize' Nampol, improve its public image and shift its focus from counter-insurgency to crime prevention.

THE ECONOMY

In his inaugural policy statement in March 1990, President Nujoma assured his people that the inequalities created by the 'apartheid regime' would be redressed. This would, however, not be done by large-scale nationalization (for long a cornerstone of Swapo policy) but through the relatively free play of market forces.

The priorities are those of many other developing Third World countries: to attract foreign investment (strenuous efforts are being made to create a favourable investment climate), to stimulate growth, to break the poverty cycle, create jobs and raise the standard of living. The task is not easy, for despite its substantial mineral and marine resources, Namibia is a poor country, its population too small to provide a wealth-generating internal market, the land too harsh and unforgiving to offer more than a bare subsistence living to most of the people.

Namibia depends heavily on three major industries – farming, mining and fisheries, which between them accounted for about 40,4 per cent of the gross domestic product (GDP) in 1989.

Agriculture contributes around 11 per cent of GDP. Cattle-ranching (the national herd numbers just over 2 000 000 head) and raising karakul and other sheep (3 000 000 head) are the principal commercial activities. At the time of independence in 1990 these activities were largely controlled by white interests. About 2 000 000 goats, most of them owned by peasant farmers, graze the sparse pastures. Nearly 70 per cent of the economically active population are employed on the land.

Much of the country's food needs (in particular that of the semi-arid southern region), including grains, fruit and vegetables, has to be imported from South Africa. The northern regions are more generously endowed, the comparatively well-watered and fertile land yielding maize, millet, sorghum and groundnuts, amongst others.

Mining accounts for approximately one third of GDP and for some 80 per cent of the value of export sales. The industry is based on diamonds – mined along the barren southwestern seaboard by CDM, a subsidiary of the international De Beers conglomerate – and to a lesser degree on uranium oxide (5 000 tons a year) and copper (35 000 tons). The million or so carats of gem-quality diamonds produced annually represent, in value terms, 40 per cent of the country's total mineral sales.

Other minerals produced include lead (approximately 35 000 tons), zinc (40 000 tons), granite and marble (18 000 tons), salt (135 000 tons), gold (1 600 kilograms) and silver (90 tons).

In geological terms, though, Namibia remains under-explored and under-exploited, mainly due to the reluctance of foreign investors to risk capital during the troubled years before independence. Deposits of coal, iron ore, base metals and gold are believed to lie beneath the ground in the remoteness of the Kaokoveld to the northwest and a large graphite orebody has been located in the Otjiwarongo district and is under investigation by Rössing Uranium.

Even more exciting are the prospects for large-scale production of hydro-carbons: the Kudu gas field off the Orange River mouth has estimated reserves of four to sixteen trillion cubic feet. Various oil deposits along the northern shorelines are soon to be explored by foreign companies under licence. A Taiwanese corporation is to drill exploratory wells inland, in the Etosha Pan area.

Fishery products have in the past contributed substantially to Namibia's total export sales, but over-exploitation has depleted marine resources and the industry is in decline. The government, however, embarked on a systematic recovery

Opening up the diamond fields: part of CDM's pioneer workings in the desolate Sperrgebiet.

programme in the late 1980s, extending territoral waters to 200 nautical miles and introducing strict quota and other conservation measures. At that time (1987) the gross catch totalled 480 000 tons, the bulk consisting of anchovies (377 000 tons), pilchard (64 000 tons) and mackerel (34 000 tons).

Manufacturing. High input costs and low demand from the small and widely dispersed population impose severe limitations on the manufacturing sector, which accounts for approximately 4,85 per cent of GNP. What activity does take place revolves around the processing of fish and beef for export. Among the other, far smaller subsectors are food and beverages, wood, metal and chemical products, and printing and publishing.

Community services

Transport. Namibia has about 60 000 kilometres of roads, 10 per cent of which are tarred. The country's principal highway, is that which connects South Africa's Cape Province in the south with Keetmanshoop, Windhoek and points farther north – it is tarred for most of its length. A good road leads from Windhoek through the desolate reaches of the Namib to Swakopmund and Walvis Bay on the coast.

Generally speaking, the huge distances and the enormous cost of road development have tended to place the emphasis on air services. Windhoek's airport falls into the international category and many of the smaller centres boast airfields, seven of which offer scheduled flights. The national carrier is Air Namibia.

The railway system comprises just under 2 400 kilometres of track, along which some 5 000 000 tons of freight are carried each year.

Media. Namibia has a lively, refreshingly outspoken press; in 1990 there were five daily and three weekly newspapers. Radio (250 000 receivers) and television (30 000 receivers) services are reasonably well developed.

Health and education. Both these sectors are receiving priority attention from a government acutely conscious of the country's long-term needs.

Namibians have a Physical Quality of Life (PQL) index of 64 (100 is the perfect rating). The PQL is derived from a number of elements such as adult literacy rates, infant mortality and life expectancy which are combined to form a model (created by the Overseas Development Council) that indicates the extent to which human needs are met by society. Currently Mauritius enjoys the highest ranking in Africa (84), followed by the Seychelles and South Africa. Namibia ranks ninth.

Just prior to independence in 1990 there were about 280 physicians in public employment or private practice – one for every 4 450 Namibians. Hospital beds total 7 540, or one for every 166 persons; infant mortality is running at 120 per thousand live births; and life expectancy per live birth is 50 years (up from 44 years in 1970). The picture is a lot brighter when it comes to nutrition: the daily per capita calorie intake has been estimated at 1 197, or 96 per cent of the FAO's recommended minimum requirement.

There have been impressive advances in the sphere of primary education: around 60 per cent of the labour force had no formal schooling in 1977, and most of the remainder had only a primary education. Ten years later, by contrast, 75 per cent of the total population over 15 years of age was classed as functionally literate. Primary enrolment had climbed to 281 000 and secondary to 83 000. In addition, there were five vocational and teacher-training colleges and one tertiary institution, which now has university status.

Tourism

Namibia has enormous tourist potential, and now that the bloody insurgency war has been brought to a close and the northern areas opened up, this can be developed to the full. The country's principal drawcards are its excellent hotels, restaurants and shops, its fascinating diversity of peoples, its splendid game parks and private game lodges, its unique floral heritage and wildlife, and the haunting beauty of an immense, strange and empty land.

1	2	3
4		5
6		7

1. The run-up to independence: a United Nations (Untag) contingent arrives at Windhoek airport.
2. A UN mobile monitoring group on duty at a rural polling station.
3. Untag's Martti Ahtisaari and General Prem Chand speak to the international press corps.
4. Swapo's Sam Nujoma, elected Namibia's first president in March 1990, acknowledges the cheers.
5. Distinguished visitors arrive for the independence celebrations.
6. Namibia's national colours brighten Windhoek's streets and stadium on independence day.
7. Queen Elizabeth II on her first visit to Namibia, youngest member of the Commonwealth, in 1991. (photo: Argus Africa News Service).

BELOW: *Emblem of freedom: newly independent Namibia's multi-coloured national flag.*

Windhoek, Namibia's capital city, was founded in 1890 by a party of German military colonists, on a site that the local Khoikhoi people called Aigams, which translates as 'fire waters' - a reference to the hot springs that gush in the vicinity. The area had in fact been occupied long before then - by the Khoi and Herero and, from 1840, by the aggressively acquisitive Nama chieftain Jonker Afrikaner and his followers, who called the place Winterhoek. In 1880, after decades of bloody warfare with their Herero neighbours, the Nama finally abandoned their settlement. Ten years later a German force of Schutztruppe, led by Major Curt von Francois, arrived to keep the peace in a still-troubled region, to establish the colonial presence, and to build a fort. The latter, known as Alte Feste ('old fort') survives as the historical section of the State Museum.

LEFT: *Modern buildings flank handsome relics of the colonial past along the broad sweep of Independence Avenue (formerly Kaiserstrasse).*

ABOVE: *A bird's-eye view of Windhoek. The city lies 1 680 metres above sea level in an acacia-wooded glen surrounded by rocky hills. One of the headwaters of the Swakop River rises in the area.*

ABOVE: *German colonial edifices grace Windhoek's main thoroughfare. Most prominent of the city's historic buildings are probably the so-called Tintenplast, or 'palace of ink' (the early administrative headquarters), and the three castle-like residences – Heinitzburg, Schwerinsburg and Sanderburg – that were built in the early 1900s in the hills that overlook the leafy suburb of Klein Windhoek.*

LEFT: *Part of Windhoek's street market where shopping is an exciting experience.*
OPPOSITE: *Christuskirche, the city's gabled and tall-steepled Evangelical Lutheran church, consecrated in 1910.*

RIGHT: *Locals relax in one of Windhoek's pleasantly informal beer gardens. A substantial number of the Namibian capital's 150 000 residents are of German extraction, and much of the early past remains, most obviously discernible in the city's architecture and in the lifestyle of its colonially descended community. Among Windhoek's attractions are German delicatessens and bakeries, superb locally-brewed beer and the lively German-style carnival held each year.*

BELOW RIGHT: *Windhoek's population is drawn from a dozen different cultures, but ethnic distinctions are fast disappearing. This attractive threesome personifies modern Namibia.*

OPPOSITE, TOP LEFT: *A doll-maker, dressed in customary Herero garb, offers her wares for sale outside the luxurious Kalahari Sands Hotel.*

OPPOSITE, TOP RIGHT: *A street mural - painted in 1990, at the time of independence - in Katatura, a sprawling suburb to the north-west of central Windhoek.*

OPPOSITE, BOTTOM LEFT: *An open-air display of 'ethnic' tee-shirts.*

OPPOSITE, BOTTOM RIGHT: *One of the stalls at the Namibia Crafts Centre in Windhoek.*

34

ABOVE: *The confident face of the future. Namibia is making rapid strides in the sphere of education: in the late 1970s fully 60 percent of the workforce had no formal schooling; today well over three-quarters of the population over 15 years of age is classed as functionally literate. Jobs in the formal sector, though, remain scarce.*

OPPOSITE: *A Herero woman smiles a welcome from the entrance of her house in Dordabis, a village to the south-east of Windhoek. The area is known for fine karakul carpets, which are woven on the nearby farm, Ibenstein.*

Among the impressive bequests of Namibia's colonial past are several fortresses built, both at Windhoek and in the remoter areas, for the defence of the early German settlers. The Herero and Nama peoples, in particular, bitterly resented the loss of their land and the erosion of their age-old rights, and took up arms against the invaders.

RIGHT: *The Rider Memorial in front of Windhoek's Alte Feste. The splendid equestrian statue, the work of Adolf Kürle, was unveiled in January 1912 in commemoration of German soldiers killed in the Herero and Nama wars. Some 65 000 of the 80 000-strong Herero group died during the conflict.*

LEFT: *Schwerinsburg Castle, Windhoek, built in 1894, was an extension of an earlier fortification that had also served as a tavern.*
ABOVE LEFT: *Sailing on the still waters of Goreangab dam north-west of Windhoek.*
ABOVE RIGHT: *The rest-camp in the green and pleasant Daan Viljoen game reserve, a 5 000-hectare area in the Khomas Hochland hills some 21 kilometres to the west of Windhoek. The camp offers bungalows, a camping and caravan ground, restaurant and swimming pool; wildlife includes blue wildebeeste, Hartmann's mountain zebra and a great many bird species.*

Mining accounts for about a third of Namibia's gross domestic product and for most of the country's exports. Major minerals are diamonds, copper, gold and uranium; lesser ones include lead and zinc, silver, granite, marble and salt.

ABOVE: A giant Wabco haul truck carries a load of ore from the Rössing open-pit uranium mine east of Swakopmund.

ABOVE RIGHT: Thickening tanks at the Rössing mine, one of the largest uranium workings in the world.

BELOW RIGHT: Salt works near Walvis Bay.

OPPOSITE, ABOVE LEFT: Lead smelting at the Tsumeb Mining Corporation's plant. The area's giant 'pipe' contains more than 200 different minerals.

OPPOSITE, ABOVE RIGHT: Cleaning a gold bar at the Navachab workings near Karibib. The open-cast mine came on stream in 1989.

OPPOSITE, BELOW: Tsumeb's mine and part of the pleasantly tree-shaded town. Nearby is the famed Otjikoto Lake, a natural sinkhole into which Germans troops dumped weapons and ammunition prior to their surrender in 1915.

Namibia's 30 000-strong Baster community, most of whom live in and around Rehoboth to the south of Windhoek, are descended from racially-mixed, Afrikaans-speaking groups of immigrants who arrived from the Cape Colony in the 1860s.

ABOVE LEFT: *A mule-cart winds its leisurely way through Rehoboth.*

ABOVE: *Rehoboth's Lutheran church. Like many other Namibian towns, Rehoboth developed around a mission station.*

BELOW LEFT: *A young Baster woman takes home her load of precious firewood.*

OPPOSITE: *Two children of Rehoboth.*

PREVIOUS PAGE: *Summertime rain clouds gather over the grasslands of south-central Namibia. The country's mean annual rainfall is about 250 mm, but the figure is deceptive as much of the moisture is lost through evaporation. The rains also tend to be irregular, some areas receiving their full yearly quota in a single cloudburst.*

The Kalahari Gemsbok National Park lies along the country's south-eastern border. Though the park itself is in South Africa, the semi-desert savannah extends well into Namibia; the Mata Mata camp, close to the frontier, is accessible from Windhoek and Mariental.

RIGHT: *A young white-faced owl (Otus leucotis) of the Kalahari.*

CENTRE: *A ground squirrel (Xerus inauris) takes an upright stance while feeding. This diurnal species, which lives in warrens of up to 30 individuals, is mainly vegetarian but does eat insects on occasion.*

BELOW: *A greater kestrel (Falco rupicoloides) surveys his desert domain. The Kalahari is renowned for its birds of prey.*

OPPOSITE: *The typical scrub and red-sand terrain of the southern Kalahari. Nowhere in the region is there any natural surface water; many of the animals rely on the occasional borehole sunk to tap the Kalahari's dry river courses; others obtain their moisture from such succulent plants as the tsamma melon and wild cucumber. Wildlife includes gemsbok and springbok, both superbly adapted to the arid environment; blue wildebeeste, eland, steenbok and such predators as the cheetah, brown hyaena and black-backed jackal. Among the 215 bird species are bateleur, martial and tawny eagles.*

ABOVE LEFT: *Karakul sheep graze on the meagre ground cover of the Aus region. These hardy animals, originally from the Bokhara area east of the Caspian Sea, were introduced into Namibia in 1907 and have since become a mainstay of the country's farming economy.*
ABOVE: *Sunset over Hardap Dam, west of Mariental and Namibia's largest reservoir. The recreation resort is a popular venue for fishing, sailing and windsurfing.*

ABOVE: *This unusual row of giant palm trees is a prominent landmark in the Stampriet area, on the upper reaches of the Auob River some 60 kilometres north-east of Mariental. The village of Stampriet takes its name from the reed-fringed natural springs that were once a feature of the region. Underground water is now harnessed, through a series of strong-flowing artesian wells, to nurture fine crops of maize and lucerne.*

47

ABOVE: *A pair of rosy-faced lovebirds (Agapornis roseicollis) in their tree-top domain. In spring, when their favourite seeds are ripening, these colourful residents of the drier regions gather in flocks of hundreds.*

RIGHT: *The long and lonely road between Keetmanshoop and Grünau, a junction that serves as the departure point for the Kalahari Gemsbok National Park to the east. To the west of Grünau is the Fish River Canyon.*

OPPOSITE, ABOVE: *The town of Keetmanshoop, a major road and rail junction some 480 kilometres south of Windhoek. Karakul sheep farming is the mainstay of the local economy.*

OPPOSITE, BELOW: *The quiver tree or kokerboom (Aloe dichotoma), one of Namibia's more striking tree species, is a hardy, smooth-trunked plant that stores water in its succulent leaves. The early San (Bushman) people fashioned quivers from its branches. The Kokerboom Forest 14 kilometres outside Keetmanshoop has been declared a national monument.*

LEFT: *The Fish River Canyon, one of the subcontinent's most spectacular natural formations, slices through the desolate Namibian landscape north of the Orange River. The gorge, 161 kilometres long and almost 27 kilometres wide, is second in size only to Colorado's Grand Canyon.*

ABOVE LEFT: *The Ai-Ais ('hot-hot') mineral springs and resort, at the southern end of the canyon, play host to holidaymakers and intrepid hikers during the cooler winter months. The therapeutic spring-waters emerge at a constant 60° C.*

ABOVE RIGHT: *The sun-loving rock hyrax, or dassie (Procavia capensis), one of the canyon's more common residents. These small, thick-furred, rodent-like mammals are, despite the difference in size, thought to be the elephant's closest relatives.*

PREVIOUS PAGE: *The golden grasslands of south-central Namibia.*

Sunset in the blistered harshness of the southern interior. Here, only the hardiest of grasses and shrubs will grow.

Far horizons - and a haunting beauty that seduces the senses, living in the memory long after the journey is done.

LEFT: *An oasis in the wilderness: the green and pleasant vineyards of Noordoewer ('north bank') on the Orange River in the extreme south of Namibia.*
ABOVE: *Gemsbok race across the sandy reaches of the Orange River. These tough animals are superbly adapted to desert conditions: they obtain much of their moisture from the Namib's wild melons; their silvery coats reflect the sunlight; and the vessels in their muzzles help cool the blood.*

Consolidated Diamond Mines' huge alluvial workings, concentrated in the Sperrgebiet ('forbidden territory') along the southern seaboard between Lüderitz and Bogenfels, produce over a million carats a year. Most of the diamonds are found on the bedrock, which can lie up to 15 metres beneath the sandy surface.

LEFT: Portrait of a diamond miner. Many CDM employees are contract workers from the northern Ovamboland region.

BELOW LEFT: Once the overburden has been cleared, teams of workers move in to brush the exposed bedrock.

OPPOSITE, ABOVE: A giant Caterpillar scraper at work removing overburden on a section of the Oranjemund mine. CDM's fleet of earth-moving vehicles clear away some 70 million tons of sand each year.

OPPOSITE, BELOW: The glittering prize: part of a week's production on the CDM fields. The sorting process begins at the diggings, where the industrial-type diamonds - the majority - are separated from those of gem quality.

OVERLEAF: The southern Sperrgebiet, part of what is thought to be the world's most ancient desert.

Among the most evocative of the southern Namib's attractions are several isolated ghost towns, forlorn legacies of the early diamond days. In the years prior to the First World War - before the deposits became depleted and mining operations moved to the richer fields around Oranjemund - they were thriving little centres of solid houses and pretty gardens, of shops, theatres and wine cellars, of music and laughter. Today they stand silent, half-buried by the drifting sands of the desert.

LEFT: An abandoned house in Pomona, home of a long-forgotten mining executive.

BELOW LEFT: Pomona's cemetery, perhaps the world's loneliest.

BELOW RIGHT: The sagging interior of Elizabeth Bay's recreation hall.

OPPOSITE: Kolmanskop, most celebrated of the ghost towns, once boasted a butchery and bakery, a lemonade factory, a hospital, four skittle alleys, a theatre and a dance orchestra. Visitors to the country tend to bypass Kolmanskop and its smaller cousins – they lie within the 'forbidden territory' (a permit from the mining company is required) and remote from the main routes. There are plans, though to promote them as tourist attractions.

ABOVE: *A chilly sea-mist wreathes the wreck of an old diamond-dredger. Many of the diamondiferous gravel deposits lie beneath the sea, but the currents and the jagged submarine rock formations make underwater mining a hazardous business.*

OPPOSITE: *The strangely eroded Bogenfels rock arch, a striking feature of the southern Namib shoreline. It rises a full 60 metres above the often turbulent Atlantic waters. A dare-devil pilot is said to have flown through the arch.*

ABOVE: *The Sperrgebiet coast is home to a myriad seabirds, including large colonies of Cape cormorants.*
RIGHT: *Flamingoes in flight close to the shoreline.*
OPPOSITE: *Few of the world's coasts are as bleakly inhospitable as that of the southern Namib, but the nutrient-rich offshore waters, cooled by the upwelling of the Benguela current, support a wealth of marine life. Over-exploitation of the fishing grounds, however, has led to serious depletion of the shoals.*

ABOVE: *Jackass penguins (Spheniscus demersus), so called for their loud, harsh, braying call.*
RIGHT: *Sinclair Island, just three hectares in extent and home to a huge colony of Cape cormorants.*
RIGHT, BELOW: *Cape fur seals also proliferate along Namibia's seaboard and on its offshore islands. They are regarded by some experts as a threat to the country's dwindling marine resources, and the colonies are periodically culled.*
OPPOSITE: *Plumpudding Island, one of several quaintly named guano islands in the general vicinity of Lüderitz Bay. Guano - the droppings of countless seabirds - was intensively exploited well before the colonial era; at the peak of the 19th-century 'guano rush', little Ichaboe played host to 400 sailing ships and a work force of over 6 000. Today most of the guano is harvested from artificial platforms.*

ABOVE: *The Diaz Cross at Lüderitz commemorates one of Europe's first contacts with the south-western African coastline.*
ABOVE LEFT: *One of Lüderitz's attractive colonial-style houses.*
LEFT: *Gulls and white-breasted cormorants feature prominently in the bird life of the Lüderitz area. In the background are two of the local fishing fleet's trawlers; pilchards and rock lobster are major catches.*
RIGHT: *Lüderitz, Namibia's principal port and headquarters of the national fishing fleet. The town, build around a beautiful embayment, was founded by Adolf Lüderitz, a 19th-century German trader with leanings towards empire-building.*
OVERLEAF: *Hardy camelthorn trees flourish in the Koichab pan, north-east of Lüderitz.*

ABOVE: *Hartmann's mountain zebra gallop across the gravel flatlands of the Namib-Naukluft Park. Most of the region's zebra live on the high and, for visitors, barely accessible plateau that tops the Naukluft hills, but they periodically migrate into the spreading plains of the west.*
OPPOSITE: *One of a number of wrecks to be seen beached on the drifting sands of the central Namib shoreline.*

ABOVE: *The little Cape or silver fox (Vulpes chama), an attractive resident of the Namib and its western seaboard. It feeds on ground-roosting birds and their eggs, small rodents, rock-rabbits, carrion and insects.*
RIGHT: *A dune near Sossusvlei in the Namib-Naukluft park, photographed in the early evening. At other times of the day these mountains of shifting sand take on different hues: ivory-white, golden, orange, ochre and, at first and last light, a deep maroon.*

LEFT: *The harsh grandeur of the Namib-Naukluft park, a vast, 23 400 km^2 expanse of desert which, together with the adjoining 'Diamond Area', forms one of southern Africa's largest blocks of conservation land. Most of the park comprises a vast 'sea' of sand-dunes cut through by flat valleys and the occasional dry but well-wooded river bed.*

ABOVE LEFT: *A lonely camel-thorn acacia tree is dwarfed by the immensity of a sand-dune. Some of the shifting dunes near Sossusvlei are thought to be the highest in the world.*

ABOVE RIGHT: *The entrance to the Namib-Naukluft at Sesriem, on the southern boundary of the park. The Sesriem rest camp and camping site can, between them, accomodate 500 people. Nearby is the narrow Sesriem Canyon, a rocky gorge carved out of the Namib by the Tsauchab River. The name is a reference to the six oxhide thongs which were once used to lower a bucket to the pool below.*

ABOVE: *Vast seas of sand cover much of the central Namib region. The land appears to be lifeless but is in fact home to an intriguing array of small creatures ranging from beetles and termites to lizards and snakes. The insects feed on particles of vegetation blown in by the desert wind, and in turn provide food for the larger species. Moisture is provided by fog and dew which precipitate on the scant dune grass.*

LEFT: *Two Onymacris bicolor beetles. The male rides piggy back on the female to reflect some of the sun's rays from her and so conserve her body moisture - a unique adaptation to the arid environment.*

FAR RIGHT: *A sidewinding adder (Bitis peringueyi) makes its convoluted way over the hot desert. These reptiles catch their prey by ambush, hiding just beneath the surface with only their prominent eyes protruding.*

ABOVE: *Lesser flamingoes rise from the waters of Sandwich Harbour, south of Walvis Bay. The lagoon, 20 km² in extent and accessible only by four-wheel-drive vehicle, was once a deepwater anchorage of some note, much used by the early whalers and trading vessels. Today the mouth has silted up and little is left of man's activities. The ecologically fragile area may only be visited by permit.*

The vast Namib-Naukluft Park extends inland from the southern and central coasts, covering nearly 24 000 km^2 of arid desert terrain. Only a small portion of the park is comfortably accessible to the general public, for whom three camping sites have been established. The region is bisected by the invariably dry Kuiseb River (though there are standing pools of water in its celebrated canyon), south of which are the great, shifting sand-dunes. North of the Kuiseb sprawls an immense plain of gravel whose flatness is relieved by the occasional wooded river-bed and rocky hill. Among the park's larger animals are zebra and hyaena, gemsbok, springbok, and other antelope.

ABOVE: *Great numbers of Cape gannet (Sula capensis) gather along the coast to fish, and to breed on the offshore islands. Their nests are simple scrapes in the ground; the female produces a clutch of a single large egg.*
LEFT: *The immense, sculpted terraces of the central Namib's shoreline.*
PREVIOUS PAGE: *A view of the Namib from the Kuiseb Canyon, through which the Kuiseb River passes on its way from the central highlands. This prominent watercourse, the largest to cross the Namib even though it is dry for most of the time (its waters reach the sea only during the rare floods), acts as a barrier to the encroaching sand dunes of the south.*

Walvis Bay, previously a South African enclave, is the region's largest port and fishing harbour – at one time it boasted ten whitefish and pilchard factories. Over-fishing made serious inroads into the country's marine resources and the industry went into a decline, but a systematic recovery programme in the late 1980s extended territorial waters to 200 nautical miles and introduced strict quota measures. At that time the national catch was averaging half a million tons a year.

TOP: *Pilchards fill the hold of a fishing trawler.*

ABOVE RIGHT: *Home from the sea: a trawler skipper relaxes in harbour.*

BELOW RIGHT: *Inside a Walvis Bay canning factory.*

OPPOSITE: *A sturdy fishing boat, built to withstand often heavy seas, prepares to put out. Walvis Bay's harbour is a well-protected anchorage, one of the very few along Namibia's 1 500-kilometre coastline.*

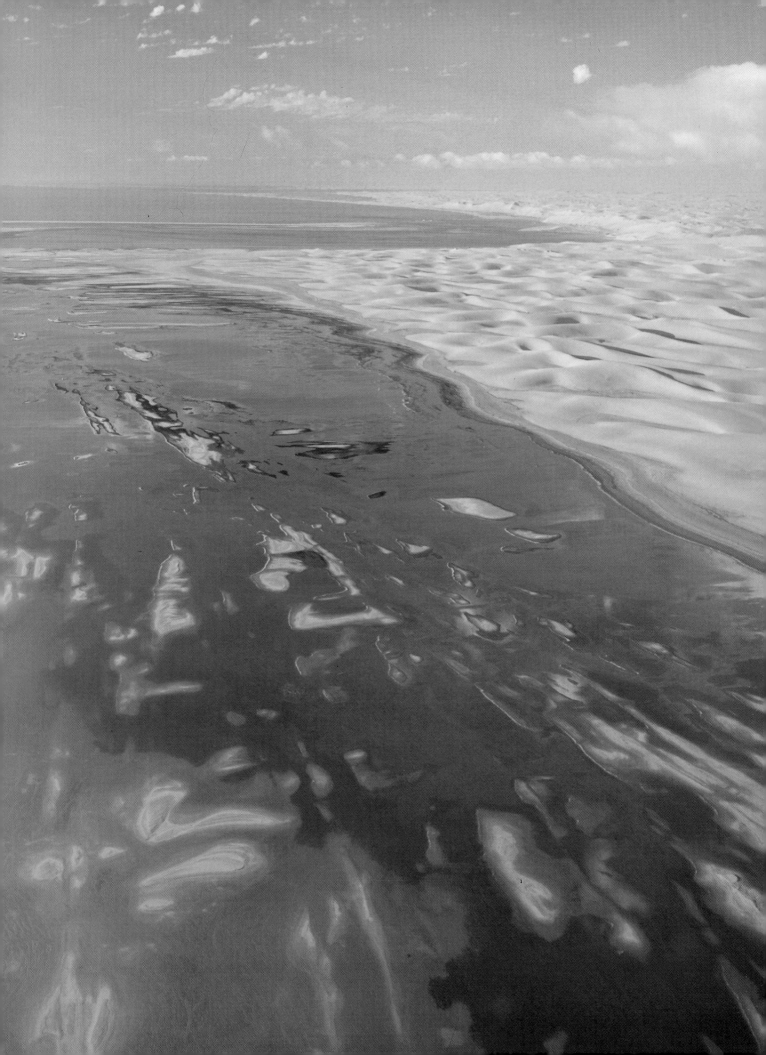

ABOVE: *Pelicans and Hartlaub's gulls congregate in a desert vlei outside Walvis Bay. The area's wetlands - lagoon, inter-tidal zone and salt workings - are ranked among the southern hemisphere's most important for migratory shore birds, including sandpipers, grebes and plovers. Around half the world's chestnut-banded plovers make their homes here.*

OPPOSITE: *The shallow waters of an extensive lagoon probe into the central Namib wasteland. These inlets are few, but the small invertebrates and algae they contain nurture great numbers of flamingoes and other waterbirds.*

LEFT: *The war memorial in Swakopmund's pleasant municipal gardens and, in the background, the 11-metre-high lighthouse that dates from 1902. Swakopmund is not blessed with a natural harbour, but it nevertheless started life as a port: the German colonists badly needed access to the interior from this part of the coast and, since Walvis Bay had already been annexed by the British to the Cape Colony, they had to make do with the rather unsheltered anchorage afforded by the Swakop River estuary until the artificial harbour was constructed.*

ABOVE: *Taking in the view from the seawall.*

RIGHT: *Swakopmund lies 32 kilometres to the north of Walvis Bay and is Namibia's premier seaside resort, a pleasant place of colonial-style buildings, well-stocked shops and fine restaurants.*
The town is set, rather incongruously, between the wind-blown desert and the chilly waters of the Atlantic Ocean; amenities include a splendid stretch of beach, a large Olympic-size heated pool, an art gallery, and a fascinating museum featuring local and natural history displays.

ABOVE: *The intricately decorative Hohenzollern building, a fine example of Baroque architecture. Completed in 1906, it was originally a hotel but now does duty as an apartment block.*
LEFT: *Swakopmund's beach on a balmy day. The water is usually too cold for comfortable bathing, but the white sands beckon the sun-worshipper.*
OPPOSITE, ABOVE: *The National West Coast Tourist Recreation Area, which extends for 200 kilometres from a point just outside Swakopmund to the Ugab River in the north, is becoming increasingly popular among discerning sea-anglers who record excellent catches of kob, galjoen, geelbek, blacktail and steenbras.*
OPPOSITE, BELOW: *Holidaymakers enjoy a sunny Swakopmund day.*

ABOVE: *One of the architectural oddities of the Swakopmund area is the Burg Hotel Nonidas, some 12 kilometres east of town. The grandiose turn-of-the-century building contains much of historical interest; its restaurant offers traditional German cuisine.*

RIGHT: *In the early colonial days camels were used fairly extensively for desert transport but today survive only as tourist attractions. They are bred on a farm near Swakopmund, and take visitors on excursions into the desert.*

RIGHT: *A fine Stone Age rock-engraving at Twyfelfontein, in the central Damaraland region. The area's rock slabs provide the 'canvas' for more than 2 500 petroglyphs - the largest concentration in Namibia.*

FAR RIGHT: *San (Bushman) paintings at the Hein Cave site in the Erongo mountains.*

BELOW RIGHT: *Karibib is a welcoming halt on the long road between Okahandja and Swakopmund. The town has some interesting buildings; super-hard marble is quarried in the vicinity.*

OPPOSITE: *The stark grandeur of Gross Spitzkoppe, north-east of Swakopmund and a perennial challenge to the serious mountaineer (its summit was first scaled only in 1946). Among other notable features of the area are the dome-like Pondok mountain, Klein Spitzkoppe, a number of strange rock formations and, at the Bushman's Paradise site, a natural amphitheatre that encompasses a splendid floral wonderland.*

ABOVE: *The Skeleton Coast Park is a 600-kilometre strip of sand and gravel, dyke and rugged ravine fringed by perhaps the world's most forbidding shoreline. Nevertheless, a wide variety of animals and plants survives in this harsh land.*

LEFT: *A figurehead from an early sailing ship. The Skeleton Coast has been a graveyard for ships since the first European navigators sailed south in search of a sea-route to the Orient.*

ABOVE: *Seals at Cape Cross. The reserve is sanctuary for more than 80 000 Cape fur seals, the males of which start establishing individual territories in the latter half of October. Pups begin appearing about a month later.*

RIGHT: *Replica of the padrão erected in 1486 by Portguese admiral Diego Cão, the first European to make a landfall in what is today Namibia. The original limestone edifice, much weathered by the centuries, was removed to Germany in 1893.*

ABOVE: *The beach-combing black-backed jackal is a fairly common sight on the Skeleton Coast. Its diet includes seal pups, carrion and birds' eggs.*

The Brandberg series of massifs, in central Damaraland, rise to 2 000 metres and more above sea level (highest point in Namibia is the Brandberg's 2 579-metre Königstein peak) and its rock faces display some of the finest of all San paintings. Among these, in the Maack Cave gallery deep in the wild and lovely Tsisab gorge, is the White Lady, an oddity that attracted, and intrigued, the celebrated French archaelogist Abbé Breuil.

ABOVE: *Elvis, a chacma baboon, is counted as part of the family at the Okonjima guest farm south of Otjiwarongo.*

RIGHT: *Game viewing at the celebrated Mount Etjo lodge, 250 kilometres north of Windhoek.*

BELOW, LEFT AND RIGHT: *Giraffe on Otjiwa game farm, near Otjiwarango; and a cheetah on Okonjima, a guest farm set amid the woodland beauty of the Omboroko mountains.*

OPPOSITE, ABOVE: *Rugged sandstone formations in the Waterberg Plateau park. The reserve is haven to a number of rare and endangered wildlife species, including roan and sable antelope, wild dog and cheetah, and the only breeding colony of Cape vultures in Namibia.*

OPPOSITE, BELOW: *A caravan and camping ground beside the Von Bach dam near Okahandja.*

LEFT AND ABOVE: *Among the Namib's unique floral residents is the weird Welwitschia (Welwitschia mirabilis), described by the great evolutionist Charles Darwin as 'the platypus of the Plant Kingdom'. The species lives for a thousand years and more but in all that time manages to produce just two leaves. These grow continuously, splitting into strips, the outer ribbon-like parts withering before the onslaught of burning sun and driven sand. Some specimens reach a mass of 100 kg; all have turnip-like stems, very long (up to 20 metres) tap-roots and leaf-pores that close up during the blistering desert days.*

Damaraland extends 200 kilometres inland from the desolate Skeleton Coast and 600 kilometres southwards from Kaokoland: a huge, untamed, ruggedly beautiful region that offers the more adventurous traveller challenge and an infinity of interest. Here there are jagged mountain ranges and deep gorges, game-rich grassland plains and, towards the west, endless sandy wastes that, incredibly, are able to sustain small, but wide-ranging, populations of

elephant and rhino, giraffe and other species. These animals have adapted their lifestyles to survive the harshness of the sun-blistered, almost waterless desert spaces. Together, Damaraland and Kaokoland are known as the Kaokoveld.

ABOVE: *The ruins of a small German fort at Sesfontein, named after the six springs that surface in the area.*

LEFT: *One of the region's floral species is the colourful Hoodia currorii succulent, a member of the Stapelieae group.*

ABOVE LEFT: *Elephant on the move through euphorbia bush country. The herds of the Kaokoveld suffered grievously from the guns of poachers and illegal hunters until the early 1980s, when there were estimated to be only 70 left in the region. Strict conservation measures have since been introduced. The so-called desert elephants can travel up to 70 kilometres a day in search of food and water and, unusually, do not destroy trees in their quest for forage.*

ABOVE RIGHT: *A black rhino cow and her calf in typical Damaraland 'melkbos' terrain. The species has also been under threat from poachers.*

The Herero are an historically nomadic people, cattle-farmers by tradition and organized according to a complex system of kinship groupings rather than within a single, centralized social structure. Fire plays an important part in the body of customary belief. Many of the old ways, though, disappeared after Christian missions were established in the 19th century. Pioneers among the early preachers and teachers were the Rhenish missionaries who, led by the noted Dr Hugo Hahn, arrived in 1844.

RIGHT: *Signs of the times.*
OPPOSITE: *Herero woman and child.*

ABOVE: *Palm Sunday mass at the Orwetoveni Roman Catholic church near Otjiwarango.*
LEFT ABOVE : *Herero women in their traditional Victorian dress, adapted from the fashions favoured by the wives of early missionaries.*

The Etosha Pan, a huge, shallow depression measuring 130 by 50 kilometres, is the centrepiece of one of Africa's finest game parks - a vast 23 000 km^2 expanse of sandy soil, scrub and grassland that serves as home to elephant, rhino, giraffe, lion, leopard, cheetah, zebra and a variety of buck, including the black impala and the Damara dik-dik, smallest of all the antelope.

PREVIOUS PAGE: *The sun sets over Etosha's western parts, where much of the game is to be found during the rainy season.*

ABOVE: *Burchell's zebra at the Kalkheuwel waterhole.*

OPPOSITE: *An elephant cow with her calf at Etosha's Goas waterhole. In the dry months of winter the park's elephant population increases dramatically, to about 1 500 head. During this period the herds migrate from the waterless Kaokoveld and Owambo regions, moving back when the rains begin to fill Owamboland's pans and seasonal watercourses. In Etosha, they are sustained by natural springs, boreholes and man-made pools.*

RIGHT: *Giraffe, zebra and springbok share the gift of water at the Chudob site, an especially fine place for game viewing and photography.*
ABOVE: *A spotted hyaena (Crocuta crocuta) crosses stoney ground on its way to a kill. Contrary to popular belief, this powerful carnivore will hunt as well as scavenge.*
LEFT: *The rare black-faced impala (Aepyceros melampus petersi) is one of the more unusual, and more gracefully attractive, of the park's antelope population. These animals are most commonly seen in the Namutoni area, and especially around the Klein Namutoni waterhole.*

ABOVE: *One of the most commonly seen antelope in Etosha, the gemsbok (Oryx gazella). It is noted for its long, rapier-like horns which, when seen in profile, can appear as one (its cousin, the Arabian oryx, is similarly endowed, and may have given birth to the legend of the unicorn). The animal has been known to kill an attacking lion by impaling it.*

LEFT: *The exquisite lilac-breasted roller (Coracias caudata), one of the Etosha's 325 recorded bird species.*
OPPOSITE: *The king at rest. The indolence of the male lion is deceptive: when roused, he can show a remarkable turn of speed, covering 100 metres in just five seconds.*

ABOVE: *The curiously shaped yellow-billed hornbill (Tockus nasutus). This conspicuous bird has an ungainly, highly distinctive flap-and-glide flight.*

ABOVE LEFT: *The romantic Beau Geste-type fort at Etosha's Namutoni camp. The building, constructed by the German colonists in the early 1900s, now houses a museum. Etosha has three rest-camps; a fourth, the Otjovasandu, is being developed.*

LEFT: *Black rhino at midnight at a waterhole in western Etosha.*

OPPOSITE, ABOVE: *Game-viewing at the Okaukuejo rest camp. The waterhole is floodlit at night.*

OPPOSITE, BELOW LEFT: *Overview of the attractively shady Okaukuejo camp, where the swimming pool provides a welcome respite from the intense heat. The bungalows are self-catering and well-appointed; other facilities include a licenced restaurant and a shop.*

OPPOSITE, BELOW RIGHT: *The main lounge at the luxury Mokuti Lodge, situated just outside Namutoni's gates.*

Flamingoes congregate in Fischer's Pan, Etosha. These long-legged, long-necked, pink-plumed waders use their heavy, curved beaks to sieve the muddy water for algae and minute crustaceans. Like Etosha, Fisher's Pan is seasonally flooded and forms an important breeding area for thousands of migratory lesser and greater flamingoes. If the water is too shallow, however, and sufficient rains have not fallen, the flamingoes will not breed until conditions improve in subsequent years. Both species of flamingo build conical-shaped nests in which a single pale egg is laid. Breeding is generally synchronized to ensure that all the chicks in the colony hatch at the same time. Once hatched, the chicks cluster together in communal nurseries, and are fed by their parents until they are able to fend for themselves. Survival during the first few weeks is a race against time: the chicks must grow quickly before the waters recede or they will be taken by predators.

RIGHT: *The endearing Damara dik-dik (Madoqua kirkii damarensis). The species, which grows to a height of up to 38 centimetres, is characterized by its elongated nose (which has a hairy tip), rudimentary tail and tiny false hoof.*

BELOW LEFT: *A crowned plover (Vanellus coronatus) with its newly hatched chick.*

BELOW RIGHT: *The crimson-breasted shrike (Laniarius atrococcineus) might be expected to add a bright splash of colour to its dry thornveld surroundings, but it is a shy, retiring bird, like the other boubou shrikes to which it is closely related.*

OPPOSITE: *Black-backed jackals (Canis mesomelas) feed at the carcase of a giraffe. These common reddish-brown scavengers are distinguished by their prominent white-flecked black 'saddles' and black tails.*

OVERLEAF: *Elephant drink at Etosha's Goas waterhole. This matriarchal group is a breeding herd, in which the young are especially cherished and protected. An elephant's gestation period is 22 months. Three decades ago there were fewer than a hundred elephant in the Etosha area; today the park, in the dry season, is sanctuary for over 1 500 head. When the rains come, though, many of the animals migrate to the Kavango, Damaraland and Kaokoland regions.*

OPPOSITE, ABOVE: *Lion at a freshly filled waterhole. An average 400 mm of rain falls in the Etosha during summer.*
OPPOSITE, BELOW: *The kori bustard (Ardeotis kori) is a terrestrial bird whose markings and colouring allow it to blend into its surrounds. It does not build a nest: the female simply lays her clutch of two well-camouflaged eggs on the ground. It can take to the air, and is on record as the heaviest flying bird in the world.*
ABOVE: *A Burchell's zebra and its foals gaze over the flatlands to the north of Namutoni.*

The Etosha Pan is one of southern Africa's most remarkable natural features. Millenia ago, it is thought, the great depression was a lake fed by the waters of the Kunene before the river changed its course. It eventually dried out to become a briney plain, or 'salt desert', whose saline and mineral residues and its summer moisture attract immense numbers of game. In winter the moisture disappears to leave a hard, dazzlingly white flatland above which the air shimmers in the heat. The famed 'mirages' are at their most striking during this time

LEFT: Ostriches cluster at the edge of the pan.

BELOW: Symetrically cracked saline mud characterizes the wintertime floor of Etosha Pan.

The Kunene River bisects Angola's Bié plateau before flowing southward to form part of that country's border with Namibia, and its waters are dammed in three places to provide both territories with some of their power and irrigation needs. The general area - a war zone until 1990 - is scenically beautiful but, understandably, is not yet well developed for tourism. Travellers in this part of the Kaokoveld need to take precautions against malaria.

ABOVE: One of Kaokoveld's charming hibiscus species.

LEFT: The Kunene's splendid Epupa Falls.

OPPOSITE: The palm-fringed reaches of the Kunene above the Epupa Falls.

OPPOSITE: *Ovahimba villagers of the Etanga kraal in the Kaokoveld, a vast and forbidding territory that sprawls across the far north-eastern corner of Namibia. The large whelk shell this woman is wearing around her slender neck is a traditional and highly prized piece of jewellery.*

ABOVE: *The Ovahimba, an offshoot of the much larger Herero group, are semi-nomadic pastoralists who subsist on the milk of goats and cattle and on hardy plants of an ungenerous land. Their homes are simple, easily dismantled structures of saplings bound together with the leaves of the makalani palm and sealed with dung.*
An Ovahimba family may move house as many as ten times in a single year to take advantage of better grazing elsewhere.

ABOVE LEFT: *This man is journeying by mule through an unusually fertile patch of an otherwise dry and sometimes barren Kaokoveld. Surface water is plentiful only in the vicinity of the Kunene River and the occasional spring-fed pool.*

BELOW LEFT: *The Ovahimba disdain cheap Western-type ornamentation, fashioning their own belts and home-made beads.*

The Ovamboland region of northern Namibia is generally fertile, comparatively well-watered and quite different from the rest of the country. Much of it comprises a great alluvial plain created and nurtured by the Okavango and other southward-flowing rivers, and the flat, stoneless grasslands are criss-crossed by seasonal watercourses (or oshanas) and man-made feeder canals that, together, sustain herds of cattle and goats and harvests of maize and millet, beans, pumpkins and melons.

ABOVE: *A waterlilly blooms in still waters.*

RIGHT: *A typical oshana in seasonal flood.*

FAR RIGHT: *An Ovambo girl with her fishing basket. The oshanas yield good catches of bream and other species.*

PREVIOUS PAGE: *Cattle graze in the Ovamboland plains country.*

The relatively densely populated
northern areas are commercially
well developed, their principal
centre, Oshakati, geared to
supply the more than 10 000
small 'cuca' outlets of the
region. By tradition, the Wambo
are a matrilineal people,
succession passing through the
mother's line, and the basic
social unit is the extended
family which, in a rural setting,
has its own village, its own land
and, often, its own waterhole.
Within the village are specially
delineated areas for sleeping,
storage, cooking, eating and
working, and a 'reception area'
where feasts are held and
visitors entertained.

OPPOSITE: *Four typical 'cuca'
stores in Ovamboland. The
name derives from the very
drinkable Angolan beer sold
in the northern region
before the insurgency war.*

RIGHT: *A Wambo couple pose
for the camera. The colours of
the umbrella are those of
Swapo, the majority political
party in Namibia.*

The Kavango people live to the south of the Okavango River, in countryside that is fertile, parklike, covered by tall grasses interspersed with scrub and patches of woodland that, towards the west, thicken into forests of mahogany and teak, blackwood and mopane.

ABOVE: *A little bee-eater (Merops pusillus) in its Okavango habitat. These birds are commonly seen, in pairs or singly, along rivers and streams throughout much of sub-Saharan Africa. They tend to favour particular perches, usually on bushes or sticks close to the ground.*

RIGHT: *A woman of the Mafwe group, homeward bound with her basket of millet.*

FAR RIGHT: *A Kavango home in the western part of the region. The Kavango, numbering some 110 000, subsist on the cereals they grow, on the livestock they raise and on the fish of the Okavango River.*

PREVIOUS PAGE: *Northern landscape in the late afternoon. Silhouetted are the majestic makalani palms (Hyphaene ventricosa), which are widespread on the wide plains of the north.*

The Okavango River flows for
some 1 600 kilometres
south-eastwards from Angola
(where it is known as the
Kubango), forming part of
Namibia's northern border
before continuing across the
Caprivi strip and into the
Kalahari regions of Botswana,
where it empties into the
immensity of the Okavango
Delta wetlands. For the
Kavango and the people of
Caprivi, the river is life itself,
nurturing the land, sustaining
the herders and their cattle.

OPPOSITE LEFT: *Watu dugout canoes are used both for transport and for fishing.*
OPPOSITE RIGHT: *Cattle wade through the shallow waters of the river's edge.*
ABOVE: *A symphony in reds and golds: the Okavango River reflects the glory of the day's last light.*

ABOVE: *This warthog plays amiable host to a yellow-billed oxpecker in the Mahango game reserve. Although fairly modest in size, the Mahango's five major habitats are haven to a remarkable variety of plant and animal life, including 60 species of mammal.*

RIGHT: *The Okavango's Popa falls, or rapids, in the eastern Kavango region. A pleasant rest-camp of teak cabins has been established nearby; downstream is a more luxurious private lodge.*

RIGHT BELOW: *Fishermen enjoy their sport in the wide waters of the Zambesi near Katima Mulilo in East Caprivi.*

OPPOSITE: *Hippo are prominent residents of the floodplain's reedbanks.*

ABOVE: *Nuns of Nyangana, a Roman Cathloic mission established in the north near the Okavango River.*
LEFT: *The pleasantly embowered village of Rundu, on the banks of the Okavango and administrative centre of the Kavango region.*
OPPOSITE : *Two women of the Barakweno group of the San (Bushman) people. The Barakweno live along the Okavango in West Caprivi.*

RIGHT: *A herd of elephant crosses the flat terrain of East Caprivi. The region enjoys only moderate rainfall, but large areas are inundated, and much of the local population is displaced, when the Kwando and Zambezi rivers rise in flood.*
ABOVE: *Warning sign on West Caprivi's main highway. During the dry season the elephant make their way from Angola, Zambia and West Caprivi into the Mahango game reserve.*
OPPOSITE: *Giant baobab trees are a common sight in East Caprivi. The species lives for many centuries, its branches reaching a spread of up to 40 metres.*
PREVIOUS PAGE: *A dusty Caprivian stock kraal. Cattle are a mainstay of the local economy.*

ABOVE: *A wildlife observation boat, equipped with all the comforts, drifts on the serene waters of the Kwando River near the Lianshulu Lodge in East Caprivi.*

LEFT: *The attractive malachite kingfisher (Alcedo cristata), a common resident of the wetlands.*

OPPOSITE: *The Kwando in its East Caprivi reaches. The river rises in central Angola and flows south-eastwards to spread out into the Linyanti marshes at the head of the Okavango Delta.*

ABOVE: *The African jacana (Actophilornis africanus), or lilly-trotter, a familiar sight in the wetlands of East Caprivi. The bird's long, straight toes and nails enable it to walk with confidence on floating vegetation.*

RIGHT: *A sunset view of the floating river-bar at Katima Mulilo's Zambezi Lodge, an attractive place that offers chalets, camping site, restaurant, swimming pool and nine-hole golf-course. The village itself is a fast-developing little centre; worth calling in at are the Caprivi Art Centre and the daily open-air market. Elephants are frequent visitors to Katima Mulilo's river-bank.*

OVERLEAF: *A young East Caprivi fisherman proudly displays his catch of catfish and bream.*

INDEX